Colne Valley gravel pits

First day of spring. Magnificent bright, exhilarating, day
Clumps of bright green distance right up to the
road at Rickm. like golden rod a little. Extraordinary
contrast between pits first entirely empty, but
on Stockers Lake — Red-crested pochard (male).
Goldeneye (males displaying, plus seven females of
very varied head colour) 5 canada geese; teal,
a pair with the eye stripe and dipped yellow
tail visible far off; pochards riding close up
in the reeds + herons. A pair of
kestrels displaying, overhead. Wrens in the
reeds, gulls (common, lesser black-backed,
herring) sporting turning somersaults, siskins
swinging like budgerigars on the alder,
making a most curious dual, echoing
chink. Snipe great crested grebes, just
beginning their displays.

This hardback edition published in 2021 by
Little Toller Books
Ford, Pineapple Lane, Dorset

The Unofficial Countryside was first published in 1973
by William Collins Sons & Co.

ISBN 978-1-908213-93-8

Text © Richard Mabey 1973

Foreword © Richard Mabey 2021

Jacket artwork © Michael Kirkman 2021

Illustrations © The Estate of Mary Newcomb 2010

Typeset in Sabon by Little Toller Books
Printed in UK by TJ Books

All papers used by Little Toller Books
are natural, recyclable products made from
wood grown in sustainable, well-managed forests

A CIP catalogue record for this book is available
from the British Library

1

THE
UNOFFICIAL
COUNTRYSIDE

Richard Mabey

LITTLE TOLLER BOOKS

IN MEMORY OF KENNETH ALLSOP,
PASSIONATE DEFENDER OF ALL OUR GREEN PLACES, WITHOUT
WHOSE INSPIRATION AND ENCOURAGEMENT THIS BOOK WOULD NOT
HAVE BEEN WRITTEN.

Contents

misty

lar
sm
le
s

even s
wire

brown in
light

smaller still –
details of cobwebs as
complex in their st
as a pylon is to a

• mm in f
dk blue

feet of the big pylon

Foreword

I N THE LATE 1960s I was working as an editor at Penguin Books, out at its headquarters in Middlesex. Our newly formed education division had been given the brief of creating a new generation of textbooks for schools and universities, against a background of worldwide student unrest. I think it was the most thrilling work environment of my life. It was innovative, gregarious, wildly maverick. And, beguilingly, the landscape round the department seemed to share a lot of the same qualities. Our office was a couple of miles north of the M4 and Heathrow Airport, close to a bizarre no-mans-land of derelict canals, Victorian rubbish tips and straggles of left-over wasteland. On the surface it looked like the set of a disaster movie – except that it was brimming with life. Migrant waders dropped in at a sewage farm near the end of Heathrow's main runway. Jungles of plants from four continents grew deliriously on the abandoned tips. A great-crested grebe had built a nest in a floating car tyre on one of the still-active gravel pits. The top predator was an Alsatian guard dog.

I spent a lot of my spare time meandering about this hybrid landscape, and increasingly it seemed to be saying something powerful about the resilience of nature, and our self-serving image of 'the countryside' as the proper location of the wild. I was close to finishing my first book, *Food for Free,* and it occurred to me that an exploration of this 'unofficial countryside' (the title came easily) would be an exciting follow-up. I'd also been lucky enough to make friends and work with the writer and broadcaster Kenneth Allsop, and his jagged prose about the wildlife of the Middlesex gravel pits in the 1940s, and around London itself in the 1960s, was an inspiration.

My original plan was to write the book as a kind of travelogue, an account of a series of long walks right round the outskirts of London, starting in the west, travelling south of the Thames to Dockland and the East End bombsites, then back through the cemeteries and railway cuttings of the north. I abandoned this storyboard after the very first day. I'd seen a calling cuckoo momentarily snagged on a lido fence, but was utterly frustrated by having to negotiate miles of barren housing estates and jammed high streets. I felt lost and disjointed and very far from jostling along with a throng of buccaneer wildings as I'd hoped. So I replanned the book. It would be a set of seasonal set-pieces linked by some fairly orthodox natural history writing about the ecology of urban habitats.

But if I was setting out now, I'd have stuck with my original plan. Urban wildlife is by its very nature fragmentary and capricious. So is our human experience of it. The passages here that are first-person narrative – when I'm fully there, managing to get lost on Hampstead Heath, sinking up to my thighs in the perilous mud of the Serpentine trying to watch waders, slum-botanising with scavenging kids on the East London rubbish tips – lift the text for me now. This kind of personal narrative, a blend of observation and reflection, has become the default mode for nature writing. But back then, injecting myself into the entire story would have seemed indulgent and inappropriate.

For me, the legacies of *The Unofficial Countryside* have not just been an enduring delight in these eccentric, 'edgeland' spaces (terrain vague, Victor Hugo called them) but a relish for the incongruity they represent. Urban wildlife is essentially comic, in a Shakespearean sense. Nimbleness and versatility are rewarded. The drama proceeds through displacement, contradiction, transformation, and eventual reconciliation. It challenges the tidy categories by which we regiment the world, and thus has a very pure kind of wildness. When, a year after publication, I made a BBC film based on the book, it was full of improbable theatrical moments. A kestrel nesting in a tower block window-box. A rare African clothes moth which had escaped into Buckingham Palace gardens after a Commonwealth Prime Ministers' Conference. Two decades later I discovered the forest of fig trees along the banks of the River Don in Sheffield, where seeds from food residues had sprouted with the help of water warmed by the city's old steelworks. They seemed like an improbable benediction, something which joined the human and natural histories of the place.

As for the unofficial countryside itself, it has had mixed fortunes since the book was published in 1973. Gravel pits have become marinas, the last scrubby bombsites are buried under National Car Parks, and the Olympic project has levelled down the most characterful tangle of wet and wilderness in the East End. Spontaneous greenspace has become demonised as wasteful brownfield, and an anaemic tidiness creeps across the last fragments of free land. But in the last few years the importance of these left-over spaces has begun to be realised, and not just for the refuge they give to urban dwellers. In an increasingly unstable world, the fleet-footed and adaptable organisms that make up the urban biosphere may have a crucial, healing role in sustaining life.

Richard Mabey
Norfolk, November 2021

Prologue

Experiences have a way of staying naggingly out of focus until after you have been through them. So it was with this book, whose true beginning I only chanced upon, like a glimpse of the perfect setting for a dust-jacket photo, months after I had finished work on it.

It had been what they call a normal working day. Bitching at the office, brooding over lunch. No rhythm to set the day in order but a tense slouch at the desk one moment and tetchy to-ings and fro-ings the next. The central heating was inexorably broiling, the windows too small – not that there was much to see through them but the damp and smoky air cowling the factory blocks. Driving home in the middle of a creeping three-lane jam was about as much relief as if the office had been towed away on wheels. I was locked-up, boxed-in, and daydreaming morbidly. It was difficult to believe that there was any other sort of world beyond all this.

On impulse, I had snatched out of the homebound crawl after a few miles and headed down a winding suburban lane. It led to a labyrinth of gravel pits, reservoirs, and watery odds and ends that I had often visited during my work on the book. It was hardly the promised landscape, and the whole area was pocked with working quarries and car dumps. But in the mood I was in, just to have seen some murky water lapped by non-air-conditioned wind would have set me right. What I did find that early autumn day was, I suppose, nothing special, but it made sudden and clear sense of my whole year's exploration.

I had parked by the edge of a canal which curled around the western edge of this maze of water, and had stumped off, scowling, along the towpath. I think it was my black frame of mind that made the unexpected late fruitfulness of this place strike me with such intensity. I had never noticed before that the canal here was as clear as a chalk stream. Yellow water lilies drooped like balls of molten wax on the surface. Near the edge of the water drifts of newly hatched fish hung in the shallows. Anglers, fresh from work, were setting up their tackle on the bank, and family parties chugged past in holiday cruisers from time to time. It was a bustling and human scene, but altogether different from the daily slog I had just dropped out of, and whose dog-end I could still see trailing past the hedges in the distance.

What had begun as a nervous gallop soon turned into a stroll. My eyes began to relax a little, and following the last swallows hawking for flies over the water, I caught sight of a brilliant spike of purple loosestrife in the distance. I had never before seen this plant so deep into suburbia. The towpath itself was festooned with wine-tinted hemp agrimony blooms and when a bicycling worker bucked past it seemed as natural to exchange greetings with him as if we had been in a country lane. No matter that the place he had come from was the gaunt Water Board pumping station that stretched along the bank, looking like nothing so much as an oil refinery. As dusk fell and the warning lights on its roof began to flush the bellies of the roosting gulls, I went off home like a new man.

That homely canalside stroll was as good an antidote to the workday blues as some real and solitary countryside would have been. And better in some ways, for I had beaten off the urban stresses in their own territory and on their own terms. Yet how rarely we look to this kind of landscape for some contact with natural things. Nearly forty years before, George Orwell had stood only a few miles from this spot, and been gnawed by the seemingly insoluble conflict between his twin loves: rural England and its close but dying communities, and the new industrial landscape where the mass of people were forced to live. He wrote a poem about the place called 'On a Ruined Farm near the His Master's Voice Gramophone Factory':

> There, where the tapering cranes sweep round,
> And great wheels turn, and trains roar by
> Like strong, low-headed brutes of steel –
> There is my world, my home; yet why
> So alien still? For I can neither
> Dwell in that world, nor turn again
> To scythe and spade, but only loiter
> Among the trees the smoke has slain.

Written in 1934, it was an uncanny glimpse of many of our current worries. Yet Orwell was, as so often, too gloomy. If he was right that for most of us there is no return to 'scythe and spade', the choice was not as stark as he painted it. The trees can live next to the cranes. He forgot that their roots are not just the symbolic ones of our natural ancestry, but real ones of wood and fibre. At both levels they are a goodly sight hardier than the smoke-stained branches.

Our attitude towards nature is a strangely contradictory blend of romanticism and gloom. We imagine it to 'belong' in those watercolour landscapes where most of us would also like to live. If we are looking for wildlife we turn automatically towards the official countryside, towards the great set-pieces of forest and moor. If the truth is told, the needs of the natural world are more prosaic than this. A crack in the pavement is all a plant needs to put down roots. An old-fashioned lamp-standard makes as good a nesting box for a tit as any hollow oak. Provided it is not actually contaminated there is scarcely a nook or cranny anywhere which does not provide the right living conditions for some plant or creature.

Think of the sites inside an urban area which can provide this opportunity: the water inside abandoned docks and in artificially created reservoirs; canal towpaths, and the dry banks of railway cuttings; allotments, parks, golf courses and gardens; the old trees in churchyards and the scrubby hawthorns at the back end of industrial estates; bomb-sites in old parts of the town and building sites in the new; the sludge of sewage farms and the more elegant mud of watercress beds. Every patch where the concrete has not actually sealed up the earth is potential home for some living thing. So willing are wild creatures to make-do with even the most marginally familiar habitats, that a stone curlew, a dwindling bird of open downland and dry heaths, was once found resting-up in a children's sand-pit in Kilburn.

This book is about these areas and their wild inhabitants. I have called it the unofficial countryside because none of these places is in the countryside proper, nor were they ever intended to provide bed and board for wildlife. They are all habitats which have grown out of human need. This is a scrappy definition, I know, covering everything from a planned suburban playground to the accidentally green corner of a city-centre parking lot.

Yet I think all these places do have one quality in common, and that is that, in them, the labels 'urban' and 'rural' by which we normally find our bearings in a landscape, just do not apply. It is not the parks but the railway sidings that are thick with wild flowers. Hedgy scrub springs up and spreads luxuriantly in the waste ground between factories just as surely as it is clipped down to size in suburban front gardens. And the water, an ancient and natural element if ever there was one, is mostly in decidedly unnatural holes dug out since the Industrial Revolution. Nothing seems quite complete or rounded off. Buildings and greenery alike are liable at any moment to be levelled, trimmed, landscaped, incinerated, modernised, or just vaguely 'redeveloped' as if they were some under-used muscle.

If the ability of wildlife to survive literally on our doorsteps is remarkable, its persistence in the face of this ceaseless change is amazing. It is also, I find, amazingly cheering. For it is a bleak view to see this story as nothing more than one of survival, with Nature irrevocably opposed to Man, forever just holding on. Looked at more hopefully it is a story of co-existence, of how it is possible for the natural world to live alongside man, even amongst his grimiest eyesores.

I suppose that in the end it is an act of faith to believe that the natural world is important to us, that we need to keep in touch with life which has a pattern unshaped by human hand, with the flow of the seasons, and with things as simply brightening to a dull day as a blackbird's song and a buttercup. Yet our country cottage daydreams and passionately tended backyard pot plants suggest that it is a widely shared belief. There's a story that during the siege of Leningrad, the citizens used their furniture and even their doors for firewood rather than cut down the city's trees.

It is for this reason that I have not tried to stop this book being a very personal account. I am no biologist anyway, and it would have been pretentious of me to try and write a scientific study of biological adaptation in man-made environments. There are other things this book is not. It is neither comprehensive nor historical. The fact that polar bears once splashed about in the Thames or mammoths grazed on the site of the M1 is not very relevant to our experience of nature now. Nor have I done more than touch upon those myriads of minute creatures – microscopic insects, algae, moulds, bacteria and the like – on which the whole living superstructure depends. This natural underground will, for our lifetimes at least, be sadly beyond the ordinary view of the layman.

It is the common, everyday experience of bird and flower and tree, cohabiting with us in our urban areas, that I have tried to capture. That, if you like, is the message. The medium is an account of a year in the unofficial countryside, based chiefly around my personal observations and experiences, but organised so that some of the mechanisms of adaptation are highlighted when they seem most important.

The danger in this approach is being tempted into some biological slumming. The habitats I've described in this book are in no way a substitute for the official countryside. Nor are they something to be cherished in their own right, necessarily. The last thing I want to do is to excuse the dereliction, the shoddiness and the sheer wastefulness of much of our urban landscape.

And living with and learning to enjoy the natural world does not mean trying to copy it. The fashionable and banal practice of comparing human and animal behaviour could have some disturbing results in this context. I hope we are never forced to ape the peppered moth, which could only survive on the grime-encrusted trees of the industrial North by turning black itself. Or that like that notorious mutant carp in the polluted waters of Lake Erie, we learn to thrive on the poisons in our environment. There is now a more chilling example still. An American grasshopper living in an area heavily sprayed with weedkiller has been found to be recycling the chemical and adding it as a booster to the fluid it secretes naturally to repel its enemies. But these are all exceptional examples. In areas of gross contamination most plants and animals quite simply die. They have no choice. We do have one, which is to clear up our own filth.

It is easy to become sceptical of the ecological soothsayers when you learn, for instance, that there are twice as many birds per acre in urban areas as there are in most of the open countryside. This is not the point. Discovering that the natural world is indifferent to at least the clutter and ugliness (but not usually the poisons) of our urban environments does not mean that we should be also. We should instead be trying to make our built-up areas more fruitful and life-giving for *all* their inhabitants.

For it is nature's fight back which is such an inspiration, her dogged and inventive survival in the face of all that we deal out. It is this survival story, and what it can mean for us, that is the subject of this book.

sh
d
ghter
colour

d balls rammed
to repair
sts

the man
lad
his
hun

house martins carrying mud from the pond,

PART ONE

Spring: Settling In

Bearings

WHEN I BEGAN working on this book I found that I needed to 'settle in' just as much as the creatures I was watching. So I think I should begin by saying a little more about how, in practice, I set about the job.

The parts of the book that are based around my own observations almost all concern the outskirts of London and West Middlesex. Yet, with a species changed here and there, they could be about any built-up area in the world. It is the process that is important, not the place. But I must confess that in my desire to have specific situations to hang the story round, I had originally intended to write the book as a travelogue. I planned to journey in an erratic circle around London, tacking towards and away from the centre, backtracking after uneventful days, and lingering just as long as patience would allow until I had seen at least a couple of seasons on the way. In the end – or rather on the very first day – this proved to be a ludicrously inappropriate formula. I hope I may be forgiven taking a few pages to explain why, since the reason does have some bearing on the way one looks at nature in the unofficial countryside.

If you want to see a wide stretch of country it's difficult not to think in terms of an expedition: meticulously planned routes, survival packs on the back, evenings spent writing up notes under the Tilly lamp. I blame much of this frontiersman daydreaming on the winter, which strands you at home with nothing more than maps and check-lists to pore over. In these circumstances the prospect of striding over the summer roads – even if these are likely to be urban ringways – can be intoxicating. I spent the winter months before my trek in the belief that just by *walking* these stale and familiar landscapes I would achieve new heights of concentrated observation and insight. Blame that on Wordsworth. There was also Defoe to be reckoned with, and the memory of that great army of explorers who travelled the land on foot and horse over the last centuries, seeing 'the tour' as a neat device for weaving their thoughts and observations into a narrative.

There was Cobbett, joyous, compassionate, idealistic, who delighted in flower and flower-picker alike; the curmudgeonly Arthur Young, who was so appalled by any unclipped hedge or unproductive wilderness that he wanted the New Forest cut down for smallholdings. My own favourite is John Taylor, a roguish, mercenary, but thoroughly lovable seventeenth-century tourist, who determined not only to see England first hand, but to make his travels pay. His method was to persuade his friends to take out subscriptions in return for regular postal accounts of his journeyings (and this three hundred years before sponsored charity walks!). I feel a great sympathy with this jaunty wanderer, recalling how well I've dined myself off improbable tales brought back from rubbish tips and sewage farms.

> Like to the Stone of Sisiphus, I roule
> From place to place, through weather faire and foule,
> And yet I every day must wander still
> To vent Bookes, and gather friends good will;
> I must confess this worke is frivalowse,
> And he that (for it) daignes to give a lowse,
> Doth give as much for it as 'tis worth, I know.

> *Wandering to see the Wonders of the West*, 1649

In our own time, when more outlandish means are needed to see things with a fresh eye, John Hillaby walked from Land's End to John o' Groats without touching a major road, and the American naturalist Edwin Way Teale, making up in scale what he lost in intimacy, covered 11,000 miles of springtime Britain in his hired Vauxhall. Just to read their books had me scribbling route maps in the margins.

I did not want to travel in quite the same spirit as them. More and more they seemed to follow in each others' tracks, lured to Selborne and John Clare's Helpston, as if it were difficult to confront the modernised countryside face to face without an earlier impression to compensate for the hedgeless gaps in your own. There was no chance of my doing this, for no one had circumnavigated the built-up areas before to my knowledge. In any case it was not so much change itself that I was interested in as how the natural world made out in spite of change. In a landscape that one forever sees in snatches through car windows, a long tramp on foot seemed the most likely way to glimpse a different face.

So a tour it was to be, broken here and there by necessity, but just about continuous in length. I set out on the first leg on a damp day at the end of April. I'd worked out what I thought was a neat ten-mile hike, covering a good cross-section of the habitats I was interested in. I'd also made sure that it crossed a few scrubby places and heaths, since I felt this first day should have a seasonal air and take in some of the migrant summer warblers.

Well, by midday I'd been lucky enough to see and hear all the commoner species, some of which can only have touched down from Africa and the Mediterranean a week or so before: whitethroats, chiffchaffs, garden and willow warblers on a common, a blackcap in a borough council park. On a golf-course I discovered some petty whin, a plant like a stumpy alpine furze, whose lemon flowers have the perverse habit of turning greener the more you dry them. Later I saw a cuckoo snare itself on the barbed wire fence round a boating lake, and hang for one sickening moment like a sparrowhawk in a pole-trap. I was all set for a dramatic rescue, but happily the cuckoo disentangled itself.

A calling cuckoo caught on a lido fence. It sounded like a parable, and I was glad it ended well.

A pretty rich bag for one morning, I suppose. I had been morbidly elated by that slight wrangle between the natural and the man-made, and added a new flower to my list. The warblers' warbling had brightened up what was turning into an increasingly miserable day. But something felt wrong. To be set up for a programmed hike like this, with highspots strung out along the route, made the whole enterprise feel too much like any old country walk, which just happened to be passing through more built-up scenery than usual. Much of it was indeed so countrified that I felt I was cheating. There was heather on the paths, thickets dense enough for nightingales, and places where there was neither structure nor person in sight. And between these there were interminable trudges through shopping centres and rows of suburban villas. I had not anticipated how embarrassing it would be to wear a pair of binoculars in a busy town street. I could not raise them to my eyes without feeling sheepish and very slightly obscene. Would the constable ever believe that I was looking at a house martin's nest under construction and not in at the typists' powder room? In the end I worked out a technique whereby I carried the glasses in my hand, not round my neck, and flicked them quickly and nonchalantly to my eye as if I were taking a shufty at the weather. Such are the hazards of trying to be a naturalist in a town – and more seriously an indication of just how unused we are to looking for wildlife in urban areas.

I'm sure that in part this is a result of the tunnel vision one develops as a defence against the colossal sensory bombardment of a city street. In such an environment you may contemplate something as static and massive as a historic building, but not, without difficulty and danger, a moving bird. There are other walkers to be negotiated, traffic to be dodged (an art at which the birds you may be watching will be singularly better than you). You will be distracted by shop windows and worried about taking a wrong turning in a network of streets that look identical. It is no use bemoaning this. It is this discordance and supercharged activity that, for better or worse, gives towns their special character. In the official countryside, if you are feeling tired, you sit down where you are. In the unofficial you become as agitated as if you were searching for a loo. (What a nicely apt euphemism 'the call of nature' is.) Preoccupations and distractions crowd around you. Stand still for a moment to escape them and even with binoculars hidden and dress adjusted you are a figure of suspicion.

After a couple of hours of trying to keep my eyes off the road, I was exhausted. My prearranged route had taken me deep into what has come to be known as the stockbroker belt. Every road and path seemed to lead straight to a 'Private' sign. It was raining steadily now, and I could scarcely use my binoculars at all – not that there was much to use them on besides a few magpies working their way through the ornamental shrubberies. At five o'clock I gave in, and caught a bus to the nearest tube station.

I had learned a lesson that I would have had to come to terms with sooner or later. I was lucky that miserable weather and an ill-chosen route had forced it on me on the very first day. It was plain what I had done wrong. Rambling might be the natural way of exploring the countryside, but it was certainly no natural activity in the built-up areas. It tempts you to try and make an adventure out of something whose most important meaning is altogether more intimate and homely. If I wanted to catch that sense it would more likely be in lunch-hour strolls, weeds found in a garden corner, a bird glimpsed through a bus window. It was a change in focus that was needed, a new perspective on the everyday.

Rambling overemphasises the sense of place, too. You try to look at sewage farms and airfields on your route as if they were natural land-forms, inexorably tied to local history and geology. They are not.

They have no real, accumulating histories like forest and downland. They are grafts on the real landscape which lies underneath them. Tomorrow they may themselves lie under a new skin.

This shifting and unstable character of urban habitats was another reason why I had been mistaken in thinking too closely in terms of specific localities. Richard Jefferies saw this during his experiences of urban nature. Jefferies moved to Surbiton in Surrey in 1877 to be nearer his editors, and though by modern standards the surroundings he describes would be regarded as deepest countryside, he felt that everything he saw was brushed by the proximity of the City. The book he wrote about his stay, *Nature Near London*, was one of the first to look in passing at the confrontation between urban man and wild nature. There is one passage which, though Jefferies was describing a universal feature of the natural world, has a special pertinence to the ephemeral environments of the built-up zone:

> The question may be asked: why have you not indicated in
> every case the precise locality where you were so pleased?
> Why not mention the exact hedge, the particular meadow?
> Because no two persons look at the same thing with the
> same eyes. To me this spot may be attractive, to you another;
> a third thinks yonder gnarled oak the most artistic. Nor
> could I guarantee that every one should see the same things
> under the same conditions of season, time, or weather. How
> could I arrange for you next autumn to see the sprays of the
> horse-chestnut, scarlet from frost, reflected in the dark water
> of the brook? There might not be any frost till all the leaves
> had dropped. How could I contrive that the cuckoos should
> circle round the copse, the sunlight glint upon the stream, the
> warm sweet wind come breathing over the young corn just
> when I should wish you to feel it? Every one must find their
> own locality. I find a favourite wild-flower here, and the spot
> is dear to me; you find yours yonder . . . It would be very

easy, too, to pass any of these places and see nothing, or but little. Birds are wayward, wild creatures uncertain. The tree crowded with wood pigeons one minute is empty the next.

Nature Near London, 1879

So what I have tried to do is to explore the natural history of this unofficial countryside, what it is and how it works, not so much as an explorer as a curious passer-by. We begin again.

The earth

In a stretch of canal near my home there was a steel narrow-boat moored for most of the spring and summer. It had been used for dredging and was full of a tangled mass of silt, beer cans and bankside vegetation. No one seemed concerned about moving it and by mid-summer it was like a floating window-box, sprouting sharp green blades of yellow iris and great water grass, bur-marigold and the pink flower-spikes of redleg.

Soil will find its way anywhere and give plants a chance of beginning. It gets blown as dust between the stones in walls, wiped off shoes into the cracks in pavements. I have even seen plants growing precariously along the bumper-rail of a canal cruiser. This was no derelict boat. The owner himself had laid this well-watered seedbed by just a few too many bumps into the side.

The earth, like so much else in the built-up areas, is rarely left in peace. Even when it is not actually concreted over, it is in a state of constant upheaval. A row of back-to-backs may be bulldozed down, the ground allowed to go wild for a year or two, then be rolled flat for a trunk road, and finally neatly hoed round the edges for the borough council's dahlia beds. In rubbish tips the ground is often worked over every few months. Soil is not for growing things in built-up areas. It is an all-purpose packaging material. You can sink foundations in it or cover up coffins. It is just earth, not *the* earth.

It would seem a dismal prospect for any living creature that depends on a settled home and a regular food supply. Yet such is the variety and rigorous economy of natural life that few nesting sites or food sources go untapped for long, and even these turbulent patches of ground have their own thriving communities. One summer a colony of sand martins cashed-in on a temporary sandbank which had been raised by a huge roadworks in Middlesex. The contractors were building a roundabout on a busy arterial road that ran up a hill covered with a light sandy soil. They had cut into the hill and exposed a face about 20 yards long and 10 feet high. This operation, I suppose, was complete in February. By mid-April, about a dozen pairs of these sleek brown birds, one of the very first visitors to arrive in this country from Africa, were starting to excavate their two-feet-deep nesting tunnels. To them this bank, about as secure as a sand-castle on a busy beach, was as good accommodation as the dry cliffs that are their natural habitat. Towards the end of June I would watch the parent birds ferrying food to their young from my Greenline, which passed within yards of the bank. Then, one evening in July, the young were out, flickering like ticker tape above the traffic jams. Two weeks later the bank was levelled off and planted with grass. I never found out whether this timing was an act of kind-heartedness by the builders or just a happy accident. It seemed a tiny miracle whichever it was, this home for a season in a substance that is a symbol for change and insecurity.

But it is the plant world that has evolved the most resourceful adaptations to these disturbed and transient habitats. Consider for a moment the qualities a plant needs to thrive in these conditions. It must, first and foremost, be a quick grower. If it is to survive it must have reached some sort of maturity before the park-keeper's hoe or earth-shifting machinery reach it. This may mean it has developed an intricate root system, beyond the reach of either, from which new plants can grow. Or it may produce huge numbers of seeds which germinate quickly and swamp any competitors. The seeds may have techniques for travelling long distances, or be capable of surviving dormantly under the soil for generations.

When a new stretch of earth is opened up it is a gang of these fast-moving, hardy, opportunist plants which get in first. They are an astonishing group, with some of the most sophisticated and ingenious techniques for survival in the whole of the natural world. We, alas, have written them off as weeds. That they smother our garden flowers and interfere with our food crops there is no doubt. But there's a well-known saying that a weed is just a flower in the wrong place. When it is in the right place, and keeping out of trouble, a weed can begin to look like a respectable plant again, with a more than usually fascinating life-story to tell.

The most beautiful of the better-behaved weeds is without doubt the rosebay willowherb. By the end of July there is scarcely a car park border, factory edge or railway line that is not graced by sweeps of its brilliant purple flowers. In the sixteenth century, when it was a much rarer plant in Great Britain, our most vivid botanical writer, John Gerard, gave this description of it:

> The branches come out of the ground in great numbers, growing, to the height of sixe foote, garnished with brave flowers of great beautie, consisting of fower leaves a piece, of an orient purple colour. The cod is long . . . and full of downie matter, which flieth away with the winde when the cod is opened.
>
> *The Herball*, 1597

In America the plant is called fireweed, and not just for its flaming flower-spikes. It seems to have a special liking for areas where there have recently been fires, perhaps because its seeds are tolerant of soil that has been subjected to heat, and so get a hold before their competitors. Rosebay seeds also need a good deal of light before they germinate, and this may be the crucial reason why the flower was so tardy in becoming common in this country.

The first signs of an advance came in the middle of the last century, when the plant started to colonise the roadsides and railway embankments that the Industrial Revolution was laying across the countryside. A further boost came from the mass felling of woodlands during and after the First World War. But rosebay was still a scarce plant inside the built-up areas, and it was not until the Luftwaffe began ploughing up our city centres that conditions were right for its spread. Suddenly there was a vast wilderness of scorched, devastated earth, laid open to the light for perhaps the first time in centuries. The first summer after the Blitz there were rosebays flowering on over three-quarters of the bombed sites in London, defiant sparks of life amongst the desolation. By the end of the war there was scarcely a single piece of waste ground in the city that was not ablaze in August with their purple flowers.

Once it has a solid roothold there is little holding rosebay. Every plant produces on average 80,000 seeds, each one a superb example of survival engineering. If you include their long plume of silky hairs, the seeds are more than a centimetre long, yet they weigh only 0.00004 grm. The seventy-odd hairs act like a parachute and can waft the seeds long distances on the summer breezes.

You might think that in sending its offspring across the world in such numbers the plant had done enough to guarantee its survival. Yet it even has a mechanism to ensure that the seeds are drifted off the parent plant at the most advantageous time.

In damp conditions the hairs of the parachute contract near their base, especially on the outside. Consequently the parachute clamps up and the seed is grounded. Only when the air is dry and warm enough for gliding and thus the conditions are right for the widest dispersal of the seeds do the parachutes open and the seeds take to the air. On any warm day in late August or September you may meet a flock of these seeds, floating on the breeze like thistledown. Most, in the built-up zones, fall quite literally on the stony ground. More will come down on soil already fully tenanted by grasses or shrubs. But with these huge numbers of seeds on the wing, there are few patches of disturbed ground, be they building sites or roadworks, that aren't also going to get their quota.

Once a rosebay seed is settled in the right sort of soil it quickly sends out runners a short distance below the surface. And here is the plant's last trick. It does not really need those seeds. Its roots live on through the winter and extend maybe three feet each season, sending up new shoots all the while.

Not many weeds are as showy as rosebay, or have as many insurance policies to guarantee their offspring's survival. Yet perhaps more than any other common plant it shows the ingenuity of the natural world in evolving ways of continuing life in disturbed and even devastated areas. Its least 'weedy' quality is probably the fact that it grows as well in comparatively natural countryside, like woodland edges and heaths, as it does in principally human habitats. We normally only come across weeds in places where we are at work, disturbing the ground. Indeed, the reason we group together this motley collection of opportunists as weeds is precisely because they dog us in this way, nipping in behind our backs to take advantage of conditions we've created for our own purposes. They are real urbanites – fly, mobile, cosmopolitan, unable to persist in most of the places they are found without the assistance (however unwilling) of man.

Yet every wild plant must have a natural home somewhere. Many of our hardy weeds probably evolved originally where disturbance to the ground is the normal order of things – screes, glacial moraines, unstable cliffs, sand dunes. They have developed qualities which, as with the rosebay willowherb, help them take advantage of similar man-made habitats where the ground is continually being churned up, and the slow-growing, deep-rooted plants given little chance to settle in.

Many of these weeds are sprinters, passing through their whole growth cycle in the time it takes more sedate plants to push up their shoots. Under the right weather conditions a groundsel seed can germinate, grow, flower and set its own seeds adrift in less than six weeks. It's thus possible for a single groundsel plant to have three generations of offspring in a single season. Other weeds lay claim to their territory by saturating the ground with massive quantities of seed. The Canadian fleabane, another groundsel-like plant which is reputed to have been brought to Europe from America in the skin of a bird stuffed with its downy fruits, can produce up to a quarter of a million seeds per plant. In the 300 or so years since its Trojan Horse invasion, it has spread across dry waste ground all over the southern half of Britain. Some weeds survive by being completely impervious to treatment which you would think would destroy any sign of life. Bramble seeds have been known to germinate from thrown-out jars of blackberry jam, which means that they had withstood a prolonged temperature of 221 degrees F.

Weeds' seeds are always there, waiting for their chance. A break in the surface vegetation, a little light and moisture and they are away. Whilst I was writing this in January I fetched a teaspoonful of earth from an unpromising patch of waste ground near my home and stirred it up in a glass of water. When the soil had settled there were fifteen seeds floating on the surface amongst the woody debris.

Yet, tough-nuts and opportunists though they may be, weeds are nowhere without man. There is nothing which demonstrates this more vividly than the rash of grey, mealy, fat hen plants which often appear on newly-dug roadworks. Who knows how the seeds got there. Had they been waiting under the surface for this liberating moment, maybe for the 35 years for which this species' seeds have been shown to be fertile? Might they have been impurities in the grass seed scattered over the new verges? Were they stamped into the ground along with the mud of countless labourers' boots? (No joke this: that great botanist Sir Edward Salisbury once raised 300 plants of 20 different species from the dirt inside his trouser turn-ups.) There has invariably been some sort of human intervention whenever a large plant colony erupts unusually fast.

Indeed without man there would probably be no fat hen in this country at all. It has never been found growing in a truly natural habitat here and was probably brought over by Neolithic settlers. It must have soon established itself in the rough ground round their settlements, and on the patches of soil where they scratched out their subsistence crops. It's nice to think of these early suburbs giving the same sort of home to the plant as our own do. Yet it was no weed in those days. Living was too hard and food too precious to write off any plant as a nuisance. The Neolithic farmers made as much use of fat hen as they did of the crops it grew with. The oily seeds went into gruels and the leaves were eaten as a green vegetable. (It now seems that they were lucky in this rather fortuitous choice of a staple vegetable: it contains more iron and protein than either cabbage or spinach.)

But the fortunes of plants that grow in association with man are always precarious. When spinach arrived with its tastier and more substantial leaves, fat hen soon went out of fashion and was left (in this case literally) on the rubbish heap. Not that one can feel any particular sorrow for such a drab weed. It is hard even to believe that it has a history at all. Weeds are too close to us, too humdrum. We judge them by convention, not for what they are. Buttercups are admired in a grazing meadow yet hunted down with herbicides on front lawns. The notion that a plant is a weed is the most effective barrier for stopping us looking at it closely. You can walk down a town street in summer past a dozen exquisite wild plants and see not one. By rights they should not be there. They seem, to the conditioned urban eye, as insignificant and maybe as annoying as a splash of spilt green paint. The big set-pieces, the plane trees and ordered ranks of flowering shrubs, even the imperial gold and purple of the willowherb and ragwort, make sense at the frantic pace at which we take in the urban scene. But the smallest of plants, just as valuable precisely because their scale and texture contrast so sharply with those of their surroundings, are overlooked. It was this diminutive and restrained challenge to urban brashness that Jon Silkin caught so perfectly in his poem 'Moss':

> Quiet, of course, it adheres to
> The cracks of waste-pipes, velvets,
> Velours them; an enriching
> Unnatural ruff swathing the urban 'manifestation':
> The urban nature is basemented, semi-dark:
> It musts, it is alone.
> *Penguin Modern Poets* 7, 1965

Such plants need the slow look, the close-up, ways of seeing that we are not used to in places where the snatched side-long glance is the convention. There are many others: the tangled mats of mossy pearlwort growing between the paving stones, with its tiny flowers like vellum bladders; red-beaded fronds of knotgrass besieging the bases of the ornamental shrubs; perhaps a sprig of bracken in the damper parts of the gutter. My favourite has always been fumitory, that spreads its pale and feathery foliage over waste ground between May and October. So much does this plant look like a wisp of smoke at a distance that its old Latin name (from which the English derived) was *fumus terrae*, the smoke of the earth. It's a fitting description. I cannot see this flower in a dusty street and catch its feeling of lightness and insubstantiality without being reminded of hazy cornfields in high summer, the plant's home in the true countryside.

A name, a colour, a smell, a season; flowers have a potent collection of qualities to ensure that they will always be teasing us with memories of walks, meetings, childhood outings. They are charms, in both senses of the word. So finding even a weed is never simply a matter of observation and identification. It is one of association as well. It is an experience that grows in richness and complexity the more you encounter and learn about the flower. It involves the sheer physical form of the plant, its shape and colour and smell; the landscape in which it grows, what you know of its biology and the way it has been used – and abused – by man; above all perhaps the accumulating memories of places and occasions on which you have met it before.

Enchanter's nightshade is a flower you might expect to cast a potent spell. I found some whilst I was working on this book, poking out of the broken concrete forecourt of a dentist's surgery in a busy high street. It's an undistinguished plant at a distance, dull green and as stark as a fish bone. Yet look closely at the tiny pink blossoms mounted like butterflies on pins up the stem. They are formed from two palest pink heart-shaped petals, mounted around two deeper red stamens. Every time I find this plant I remember my first real botanical walk and the girl whose excitement made me begin to look at flowers in a new way, sitting in her jeans on a dry woodland track, peering in amazement at the delicate symmetry of those blooms. Perhaps it was this strange twinning in the flower that led to its magical associations, and the old herbalists' belief that it was the flower used by the enchantress Circe in her efforts to bewitch Ulysses (its Latin name is *Circaea lutetiana*). Almost every part of the plant grows in twos: the leaves in opposite pairs up the stem, the calyx, the petals, the stamens. Even the seeds are in pairs inside the egg-shaped fruit.

And here, with these bristly pods which hang from the plant in autumn, we are back in the city street. For enchanter's nightshade is not just a flower of long folk history and secretive beauty; it is also a tough and expansive weed. The surface of that seed pod is covered with shiny hooked bristles which guarantee that the fruits will stick to and be carried about by any passing animals – beclothed humans included. Not that the parent plants die off completely. During the winter their roots live on beneath the soil, and in the spring, turn their tips towards the light, garlanding the site of the original plant with new leafy shoots.

Between the wars Henry Williamson wrote a tribute to this much maligned group of plants called 'A Weed's Tale'. It was a whimsical and slightly contrived parable, but in it Williamson captured, with his masterly insight into the hidden ways of living things, the indomitable determination to survive of even as humble an organism as a weed.

Via a rook-ferried twig, a swallow's bill, and the hat of a head-scratching cottager, a dock seed is relayed down on to the cobblestones by the cottager's door-scraper. The winter rains wash it (and its accompanying film of boot mud) down into a crevice between the cobblestones, where it takes root. For seven years it fights for its life against the assaults of Uncle Joe, the cottager, who with a rheumatic hatred of zestful growth, attacks it with boot, knife, and finally, in desperation, paraffin.

The old man eventually dies, but, providentially, before the dock, which in a last unharassed gasp of life succeeds in producing a score of seeds before it too expires.

The dead seed-bearing stalk of the dock is broken off by a village boy for use as a spear in a graveyard battle. The game ends, the spear is abandoned on a mound. But next year, the rooks return to perch in the elms above Uncle Joe's grave, 'upon which were growing, as though in faithful and compassionate memory, a score of young plants of *Rumex sanguineus*.'

Within a few months, waste ground is colonised by these quick-growing annual weeds that live, shed their seeds and die inside a single season. During the first winter though, the perennial plants, whose roots survive underground even though their foliage may be dead, begin to gain the upper hand. So the second stage in the plant development of these areas is the arrival of coarse grasses, docks, nettles and thistles. Meanwhile, growing up amongst these, will be bird-sown seedlings of elder, hawthorn and willow. Being relatively slow growing shrubs, they are much less demanding of light and space than the frantic annual weeds, and can usually tolerate the tangled jungle they find around them.

The elder is a classic example of a shrub ideally adapted to the disturbed and uncertain conditions in these places (as witnessed by its ability to thrive in the scratched-up ground around badger setts and rabbit warrens). It is a phenomenally fast grower, outstripping all comparable rivals provided it has a modicum of light, water and nutrients. It's able to achieve this precocious self-inflation by, as one botanist put it, 'cheating'. The unexceptional woody exterior of an elder branch is just a front; cut into one and you will find it padded out with a spongy pith about as substantial as a cellulose slimming biscuit. It is this pith which absorbs quantities of water and helps swell out the shrub so speedily. Add to this the elder's acrid foliage, which seems unpalatable to everything from caterpillars to rabbits (sprigs were once worn as fly repellents), and the unfailingly huge quantities of seed-bearing berries, greedily gobbled and dispersed by the birds, and you have a tree which is

> a typical product of contemporary life. It is light of
> construction, cheaply and rapidly produced, short-lived
> and either quickly repaired when damaged, or scrapped
> and replaced. The more solid durable trees like oak and
> yew take time to produce and are built to last; but they are
> hardly appropriate to the age in which we live . . . and to a
> countryside constantly undergoing upheaval and change.
>
> 'Tree with a Future', G. H. Knight,
> *The Countryman Wild Life Book*, 1969

Within a few years the young shrubs will be head and shoulders above the grass, and in a decade may form dense thickets. This is the natural succession of plants on disturbed ground. But it is the fate of disturbed ground to be roughed up again, and it's not often that the scrubland stage is reached. Where it is, it is in those awkward-shaped parcels of ground – left over like a hem when the surrounding areas have been sewn up – often called 'marginal land'. These seem to be multiplying with the piecemeal extension of built-up areas: a sliver of land left over between two strictly rectangular factories, a disused car dump, the surrounds of an electricity substation. Nothing can be done with these patches. They are too small or misshapen to build on, too expensive to landscape. So they are simply ignored – at least until the bushes start shutting out the light from the machine-shop. For that spell of ten or twenty years they form some of the richest and most unpredictable habitats for wildlife to be found in urban areas. Except for the first year or so of their lives, they are truly natural. The only man-made facility being cashed in on is space. Even the trees are bird-sown natives, unplanned and unpruned.

Two stretches of marginal land stick in my memory. The first was wedged between the Thames and the advancing northern edge of the huge new South London town of Thamesmead. It was early winter and I had been ferreting round the docks and river edges with a friend, looking for the wildfowl that were moving closer to London in the wake of the cleaner water. We had had no luck peering through the knotholes in the dock fencing, and decided instead to look at Thamesmead. It was a desolate journey. The pre-cast concrete tower blocks had only been up a few years, yet they were already stained from the industrial fumes blown over the river. We failed to discover a single tree, and the only green to be seen was in the few patches of razored lawn. How exasperating the planners must find this last-ditch insistence by people for some texture under their feet that is less regular and relentless than the concrete. How much tidier and cheaper to maintain it would be if they could cement the whole area over, paint the squares green, or cushion them with dyed plastic matting!

We hurried on through the estates, past the muddy chaos where the contractors were digging in for the next instalment of this ugly living factory. It wasn't long before we found ourselves in a rough patch of wasteland that hadn't yet been visited by the bulldozers. It was a relic of the vast areas of marshland that once stretched along both sides of the Thames to the east of London. No one can have used it or cattle grazed it for generations, for it was blanketed with a dense undergrowth of birch and ancient hawthorn. We disembarked from the car and followed a crumbling metalled road deep into the scrub. The air was almost unbreathable, full of sulphur drifting from the power station directly over the river. Yet there was a sense of anticipation, of imminent life, of stirrings and activity in the bushes. Magpies were working through the more open areas, and greenfinches shuttling in tiny bands between the fruit-laden hawthorns. Once we glimpsed a kestrel, a hunched silhouette on a birch top, easing himself round to glare at every quarter of this jungle. It may have been the fading light or the grimy air, but he seemed a bird made for this place, a swarthy hawk with a bony, no-nonsense body, and none of the flashy elegance of his country relatives.

Rabbit droppings showed that creatures besides birds lived here, and we followed some of their thready tracks through the scrub. There was water too; not the Thames, but a dark, still channel curving like a moat around an old brick wall, perhaps the last remains of a riverside farm. We pottered around on the bank, as one does near water, testing the mud and making harpoons out of grass spikes. It was like a fen along the edge, thick with reeds, teasels and velvet busbied bulrushes.* There was also a plant that I had somehow never

---

* I hope I will be forgiven for using the popular name for the reedmace, as *Typha latifolia* is properly called, in spite of the confusion it may cause with the true bulrush, *Scirpus lacustris*. It seems to me one of the clear cases where a popular name gives a much more vivid impression of a plant than the 'correct' one. Apparently the confusion started when Sir Lawrence Alma-Tadema painted his famous 'Moses in the Bulrushes' with *Typha* instead of *Scirpus*.

noticed before growing in the dense grass at the water's edge. It was a member of the dandelion family and covered with bristles. What struck me most though were the alarming blisters erupting on the leaves. I wondered if these were some deformity in the plant, a kind of industrial acne brought on by the pollution in the air. But later I found that the flower, the bristly ox-tongue, carries these papules quite naturally at the base of its bristles.

It was whilst we were browsing among these plants that we became aware that the bushes around us were filling up with birds. From every direction it seemed starlings were dropping into the bushes, stacking up sometimes as many as ten to a twig and making the branches sway with their weight. Quite by chance we had found our way into the very centre of a huge starling roost. Starlings begin to gather together for these roosts late in the summer, and swelled by young birds and immigrants from Scandinavia, have been known to form flocks literally millions strong. There was scarcely room for that number here, but the starlings – plus a sprinkling of camp-following house sparrows – continued to pour in. All the birds arrived in an identical fashion. They would fly over the cluster of bushes quite fast, then suddenly stop and crumple, as if they had been shot, and spin like falling leaves into the branches. It is exactly the manoeuvre a flock of starlings often makes when it is being chased by a predator like a sparrowhawk. It may be that this is a key to these curious mass roosts. Do the birds feel more secure in these gatherings, making the old adage about safety in numbers a genuine survival rule? Yet this can scarcely be the whole truth, for a roost must seem like a well-stocked supermarket to a peckish hawk, tens of thousands of dozy carcasses crammed for the taking on the shelves.

Another suggestion about the function of the roost is that it serves as a kind of information centre. Those birds that have discovered good feeding grounds during the day circulate the news by leading the flock out the next morning. Listening to the rousing babble of these birds, which was well nigh blotting out the grind of the concrete mixers a few hundred yards away, it was easy to believe that the information was *already* being passed on. No one has ever described the starling when he is giving out this extraordinary medley of clicks, gurgles and mimicry better than W. H. Hudson:

> Watch him when absorbed in his own music, especially when emitting his favourite saw-filing or milking-a-cow-in-a-pail sounds: he trembles on his perch – shivers as with cold – his feathers puffed out, his wings hanging as if broken, his beak wide open, and the long pointed feathers of his swollen throat projected like a ragged beard. He is then a most forlorn-looking object, apparently broken up and falling to pieces; suddenly the sounds cease, and in the twinkling of an eye he is once more transformed into the neat, compact, glossy, alert starling!
>
> *Birds in London*, 1898

We were now totally surrounded by the birds, the packed terraces beginning no more than a couple of yards away from us. I think we must have seen too many Hitchcock films, for we both felt a powerful need to get out at this point, and retired to the top of a slag heap about thirty yards away. From here we could begin to see a pattern in the birds' movements. All of them seemed to be flying from the south side of the river, the water forming a natural northern boundary for this particular catchment zone. The lowest flying birds, which had presumably come from nearby, were in small groups of rarely more than ten. The highest, which may have flown five miles or more, were made up from amalgamations of the smaller bands, and some numbered several hundred.

We watched them from our perch for maybe twenty minutes, and there was still no letting up either in the numbers arriving or in the hubbub. I do not know how one begins to count the numbers of roosting birds accurately, but I can't believe that there were less than twenty thousand birds by the time we left. When we did go it was with some regret, and we paused near the car to have a last look at the roost through our binoculars. In the few minutes since we'd left the area a team of surveyors had occupied the slag heap, and were peering through their theodolites over the scrub. A few months later no doubt the bulldozers moved in and twenty thousand birds had to search out another site to spend the winter nights. They probably found this easier than the future inmates of this wing of Thamesmead will find a place to stretch their legs and catch a glimpse of one of the most exciting spectacles of British wildlife. I doubt if the starlings will ever return to roost on the bland tower blocks as they have learned to on the ledges and window sills of older city buildings all over the country. Round Trafalgar Square their dusk flights are so spectacular as they mount up suddenly from their roosts and fold like a black cloak around the tops of the buildings, that they have more than once nearly had me run over.

It's not so surprising that these birds, which in the wild nest on cliffs and in the crevices of old trees, should have found some sort of workable alternative in the craggy surfaces of city architecture. For roosting also, the higher temperatures of urban buildings must be attractive to birds which need to conserve every calorie of energy during the winter months. The preference for urban roosts seemed to begin at about the same time as the built-up zones began making serious inroads into the starlings' natural habitats, and maybe they were able to find an advantage in what at the time was a necessity. Many species of bird move deeper into the countryside when their habitats are destroyed and end up in ghettoes wherever they can find the dwindling remains of the surroundings they're used to. Not so the starling, who as late as the 1920s turned towards the city as decisively as any ambitious country boy, and improvised a habitat out of what he could find.

More conservative birds can find refuge in patches of marginal land like the one where we first found those starlings. Although it's difficult to defend the existence of these places in a time of such chronic land shortage, whilst they do survive they are oases of real and provident country. They have cover, nesting sites, unchecked plant and insect life, and are rarely troubled by human visitors.

It is amazing how romantic these pockets of ragamuffin greenery can begin to seem, nestling, like Frances Hodgson Burnett's *Secret Garden*, behind the factory walls. You may pass half-a-dozen every day and not be aware that they exist. If you fancy tracking them down, there's nothing like a train – or better still, a double-decker bus – and a town map with the unexplained spaces marked off. Simply peering round some inviting corners brought me one behind a Co-op in Suffolk, adorned with figwort and fennel, and a disused shunting yard in Hertfordshire occupied by nesting swallows.

And sometimes their inhabitants can seem as surprising and incongruous as these islands of country themselves. Later that spring I was exploring a stretch of the Grand Union Canal in West Middlesex, in an area that had once been riddled with gravel workings. At right angles to the main cut there were disused branch channels, which I suspect had once been used to carry the gravel, but now acted as little more than drains for the factories strung out along the banks. Their chief value was the part they played in a tortuous system of water that defended the land inside it as securely as a moat. The canals occupied two sides of a rough rectangle. Along the other two, and across the centre, ran tributaries of the River Colne. Between these fingers of water was a jumble of flooded pits as ragged in outline as jigsaw pieces (and which I later learned, ruefully, had been visited by a vagrant white stork just a few days before). And rising from this watery maze were the tumuli of a long-deserted rubbish dump. They reminded me of those school geography book diagrams of rock strata, folded by some giant earth movement. This was third generation wasteland, one time gravel workings, later flooded or filled with refuse, now, too daunting a prospect for any land developer, gone to scrub.

Here and there in the more open patches were some real industrial fossils, those egg-shaped bottles used for ink and chemists' concoctions in late Victorian days. There was no doubt that it was a long-neglected wilderness. To judge by the size of some of the bushes the final stage of scrub development could have been in progress for as much as thirty years. The side of one mound was clothed with dense hawthorn and crab apple, and there were blackcaps singing there.

I remember this bank well for, scrambling up it, I virtually fell into a dense plantation of hemlock. It was an eerie experience to be pathfinding through this disturbingly poisonous plant – not yet in flower but already three feet high and growing as densely as heather on a moor – knowing that a few mouthfuls of the foliage could do me in as surely as they did Socrates. But your intuition leaves you in little doubt about the poisonousness of hemlock when it is growing in these quantities. When your shoes crush wads of the leaves and stems they give off a foul and unmistakable smell of mice. But it was good to see, amongst the livid, purple-blotched stems of the 'Devil's Blossom', another flower quite indifferent to 'colde qualitie' which Gerard divined as the poison: round one of the taller stalks there was twined, in an indisputably warm embrace, the single shoot of a young hop.

There was also a scattering of bramble and thorn thickets, and every one seemed occupied by singing birds. There were willow warblers, whitethroats, a garden warbler – the last a real plummy contralto compared with the sharp counter-tenor of the blackcaps behind me. Best of all were the yellowhammers, swaying at the top of the bushes, and looking as mouth-watering as ice-cream cornets with their vanilla heads and sleek chestnut bodies.

There seemed no end to the surprises of this place. Down another sharp bank I dropped into the ruins of a canalside warehouse, from which the shiny strap-like fronds of hartstongue fern were just beginning to curl out over the water. Farther along the canal passed, ludicrously, over a tiny aqueduct. At the edge of the brook beneath I could just make out a common sandpiper, making short dashes under the overhanging grass, holding, then sliding back into its loose, tail-bobbing stroll. As soon as I came near the brook it was up and away, skimming a few inches above the water, wings bowed stiffly downwards, flicking them once, twice, gliding, flicking again, then pitching suddenly into the cover at the side of the stream, wings strained up and back and legs scrabbling forward. It would only have needed to give its shrill, ringing call, and I could have believed myself by another brook in the Highlands, where the sandpipers nest and where this migrant could well have been headed.

I don't know how long I must have been listening to the lesser whitethroat's song before I realised what it was. I had come back to one of the disused branch canals and was walking along the towpath looking at the dead fish floating amongst the surface scum. It was ironic to see this troubled water garlanded by such flourishing earth. Along both sides of the cut, in the narrow strip of land between the water and the factories, were banks of giant sprawling hawthorns. They were studded with singing birds; chiffchaffs, chaffinches, greenfinches, and a nervous marsh tit dithering in a clump of willows. I had walked maybe twenty yards on before I realised that the dull rattle coming from the opposite bank behind me was not a hoarse chaffinch.

For me the song of the lesser whitethroat is one of the most evocative of all our summer sounds, a dry, remote, inward chatter, a voice made for the impenetrable and lonely hedges that are its favourite habitat. I had heard good numbers of this bird only a week before, on a wild heath on the North Norfolk coast. It had been a bleak, wet day, shorn of almost all bird song by a bitter Easterly – which had nevertheless blown in these lesser whitethroats from their migration flights up the

East Coast from North Africa and Asia. Migrant birds always seem to sing just after they have arrived, as if they needed to proclaim a temporary resting territory after their exhausting journeys, and every hundred yards or so on this heath, a bush had come to life with a few seconds of primitive rattling. It is not easy, a few days after an experience like that, to imagine the sound in any other setting, and I think I can be forgiven my initial deafness to the bird that was now singing in a bush directly underneath an electricity pylon. Through my binoculars I could just see him working through the branches, a shifty waif of a bird with a dark bandit's eye-mask. It didn't seem surprising at that moment that it was not until the very end of the nineteenth century that the lesser whitethroat was 'discovered' in this country. He is a bird as secret and as unexpected as the patches of land that lie behind the factory wall.

The water

Water, just as much in the shape of a rancid canal as a chalk stream between two villages, marks the edges of things. It is a barrier. It keeps people in their place. To a certain extent it also keeps nature in its place, and for some plants the thinnest strip of water can prove an impassable barrier. But it is also the life-blood of the natural world, irrigating the earth, providing food and drink for birds and animals, and for other plants a carrier service for seeds. The unofficial countryside is bountifully provided with water. So much have its land surfaces been excavated, quarried, channelled and generally cut up, that towns in low-lying areas can be turned almost into islands by the water that has seeped through the breaks in the surface.

'Artificial' water of this sort – laid either deliberately or incidentally by man – usually dwarfs naturally occurring water in the built-up areas. The Colne Valley itself is a vast cone of blue on the map, four miles across at the base, and tapering upwards for nearly seven miles. It is an almost completely man-made waterscape, a complex maze of flooded pits, reservoirs, drainage channels and canals.

Gravel pits are usually the most frequent source of open water near towns, though no one has a word to say in their favour when they first arrive. As often as not the excavators carve into market garden land or a potential housing site. For the few years the quarrying is in progress the landscape looks like a bomb-testing range. The endless stream of lorries saturate the nearby houses with noise and dust, and plough up the roadside verges.

There is becoming less and less excuse for ripping gravel out of the earth in this fashion. Synthetic substitutes are being developed, and ways found of using processed industrial slag (normally just abandoned in dangerous and sterile heaps) in many of the roles currently filled by gravel. Yet these are still comparatively expensive techniques, and for a while we are likely to have to tolerate a gravel extraction industry. The one blessing is that the pits are unlikely to spread deep into open countryside. The market value of gravel is so unrealistically low that the cost of carting it more than a few miles far outstrips the cost of getting it out of the ground. So gravel is dug ('won' is the romantic euphemism they use in the trade) as far as is geologically possible where it is needed – which is chiefly on the advancing edges of big towns, with their ever-expanding housing estates and service roads. Four thousand acres of land are hacked into by the quarriers every year. But as much as three quarters of this is eventually flooded and landscaped into artificial lakes.* For unlike mineral workings, gravel quarries have the capacity to heal themselves. Most of the gravel that is quarried in this country occurs in low-lying river or alluvial plains, where the natural level of the

---

* The remainder are dry pits, where the underground water level is permanently below the floor of the quarry. These are usually filled with refuse or industrial waste, and eventually redeveloped for agriculture or recreation.

underground water is only a matter of feet below the surface. The moment the excavators dig beneath this level there is the beginning of an artificial lake.

It would be foolish to say that these flooded pits are always a gain for the landscape. For up to twenty years – the working life of a really big quarry – they are undeniably not. And even well-landscaped water can become monotonous when you have difficulty in finding a few acres of wood and field amongst it. Yet many pits, torn as they are out of monotonous rough pasture in the suburbs, have added a new element to the landscape. Such is the demand for recreational land in those densely populated areas where the pits tend to proliferate that the contractors aren't often allowed simply to desert an excavation once they've had their fill. The price they must pay for the years of noise and dirt, and for the loss of a few more acres of green earth, is to give back to the community a ready-made lake, with smoothed-down banks and freshly planted waterside shrubs. In some areas planning permission will not be given for quarrying unless the contractors guarantee to carry out this sort of reclamation afterwards. In Gloucestershire the County Authorities go as far as to specify what outline shape the pits must be dug to.

The first colonists of this waste-water are of course the water sports enthusiasts: anglers, water-skiers and yachtsmen. But wildlife hasn't been neglected, and increasingly sections of the pits are set aside as sanctuaries. If it seems out of proportion to close off whole areas of water for the benefit of a few birds (and even fewer naturalists) it's worth remembering what the most conspicuous wildlife of these places is. Ducks and the other water birds that rapidly move into the gravel pits are not secretive, specialist's birds. They are one of the most accessible and glamorous forms of wildlife we have. They court and feed out on the open water. They are large and viewable and often exotically plumaged. They are even more plentiful in the winter than in the summer. And if their relatives on the ornamental lakes are ever willing to be fed and fussed, these gravel pit birds remain defiantly and inspiringly wild. Yet even in their dramatic skidding flights about the winter sky, they are still public birds. J. N. P. Watson once called them 'the most convenient and the most delightful window to the natural world'.

The measure of protection which these water birds need most is simply some freedom from the more hectic forms of boating, and it is the banning of powerboats that is the chief provision of the sanctuary areas of gravel pits. If it's freed from damaging wash, the bankside vegetation will to a large extent take care of itself. Reeds will colonise the shallow water, and maybe help dam off small marshy lagoons. Dense thickets of alder and willow will spring up on neglected patches of ground round the edges. After only a few years a flooded pit will provide a range of habitats that are small-scale replicas of just those we are losing most rapidly in the open countryside. Although it would be silly to pretend that a half-acre of marshy ground at one corner of a pit is any real substitute for the wetlands we have lost through drainage, it may provide a home for a wintering snipe and a pair of lapwing. Even the damp scrub has its attractions. Although dwindling species like the nightingale seem unwilling to take up residence in these new wasteland habitats, others are not so fussy. The grasshopper warbler, for instance, with its extraordinary song like the whirl of a freewheeling bicycle, has undoubtedly increased in this country over recent years, and as much in these fenny gravel pit nooks as in wilder places.

Most usefully the pits have helped to add to one of our scarcest habitats – reedbeds. Once it has a roothold, the common reed will rapidly colonise the shallows at the edge of the pit, and provide a breeding site for countless insects and warblers. Anyone who is doubtful whether these prefab reedbeds can ever substitute for the 'real thing' need look no farther than the bird reserves at Minsmere and Walberswick in Suffolk, which are amongst the richest reedmarshes in the country. They look as ancient and aboriginal as the heathland that surrounds them; yet they are man-made habitats with only a few decades of growth behind them, the result of the deliberate flooding of coastal grazing marshes for defence purposes in the last war.

But the greatest success story of the gravel pits belongs to the little ringed plover. I never succeeded in finding this explosive wading bird in my chosen territory, but I have seen them at the Hertfordshire reservoirs which were their first known nesting site in Britain. They are stocky little birds, 6 inches long, with a hunched stance, beetle-eyebrows and black and white war paint that makes them look decidedly belligerent. It's an impression which is more than confirmed by their behaviour – which may be the reason they've been able to prosper in this country against almost every imaginable obstacle.

Before 1938, the little ringed plover was a very rare vagrant to this country, glimpsed on spring and autumn passage only about a dozen times since records began. But in that year a pair raised three young on the shingly edge of a reservoir at Tring in Hertfordshire. Over the next ten years, more and more nests were found, the bulk of them at the gravel pits and reservoirs that were expanding round the edge of the London area.

There is just one stage in the life-cycle of a pit when it is right for the little ringed plover. The process of gravel extraction is normally carried out by the excavation of flat terraces, from which successive layers of gravel are stripped off. When these terraces have been scraped almost to the level of the water table, a habitat exists which is very like a shingly beach: an expanse of sand and pebbles, interspersed with shallow, irregular pools. To a plover summering in Britain this is a close enough imitation of the shingly river banks that are his favourite natural haunt on the European mainland. If the plateau is left undisturbed for a year or so it makes an almost perfect nesting site for the birds. For the nest itself, a patchily lined scrape in the ground, the pebble terraces or the islands of sand near the washing and grading machines are ideal. For feeding there are the sandy edges of the pools. If these are old enough to have built up a little vegetation they will carry larvae, molluscs, caddis flies, water beetles and spiders throughout the breeding season. If not, then the birds can commute to the maturer edges of the main pit.

But it's a rare thing for a gravel table to be left undisturbed while a pit is still being worked. More often it is the actual operating surface of the pit, the very ground the excavators are cutting into and the lorries ferrying endlessly across. The plovers have to possess the tenacity of squatters defying an eviction, running a gauntlet of mechanical shovels and bulldozers, shifting their nest-site, using up maybe three clutches of eggs before they raise a successful brood. At Chingford one year, an occupied nest was found less than a foot from the regular lorry track. And if the eggs are not scooped up or run over during the week there are always anglers to trample on them at the weekend.

If the plovers somehow escape annihilation or panic, and return to the site the following year, there's little chance of it still being habitable. If the excavators have dug deeper into the table, it will likely be flooded with water. If they have abandoned it, it will not be long before the ground vegetation is too thick for the plovers' comfort. Of twelve gravel pit nesting sites closely watched in the London area between 1944 and 1950, ten were occupied for only one or two years.

Yet miraculously the little ringed plover has not only survived but spread. Eggs are hatched, young fly and each year birds return to this island from Africa and Southern Asia. By 1962 there were 158 proven nests. By 1967 (the last year for which figures were available at the time of writing), this total had increased to over 230. As the summer population has grown and pressures on the traditional nesting sites increased, so the birds have become more enterprising in their improvisation. The first pair to be found in Surrey, in 1956, had nested on top of the clinker that had been dumped inside a disused dry pit near Richmond. Recently birds have occupied open-cast mining sites, old airfields and dumps of industrial waste. It is fascinating that only at this point in their history have a few pairs of birds started to settle (almost as a last resort, it seems) in natural habitats on the gravelly edges of some of our larger rivers.

The little ringed plover is by no means the only bird to have cashed in on all this artificial water. The sheer vastness of some of the pits and reservoirs, together with the fact that geology tends to group them together into chains, means that they can serve as congregating and staging posts for birds on migration.

In the spring you can often see flocks of sand martins edging slowly across the pits, a few feet above the water, and uttering their curious bony chatter. They are midge-coursing. Yet when you see a really big squadron, tacking across the water with their heads down into the April wind, you could believe that they were on some vast trek, and that martins stretched from the pit to both horizons.

In the balmier days of mid-August it is usually the fledgling swifts which are racing crazily about the pits. Not for them the orderly quartering of the martins. They hammer after any insect that happens to be in their path. Their deftest trick is to snatch flies off the surface of the water with their bills. They arch their wings above their body, sometimes until they are almost touching, making for themselves a combined parachute, balance and brake that slows them down from 60 m.p.h. to something like fifteen in the space of twenty yards.

There are few birds of the urban areas more mysterious or thrilling than swifts. They are creatures utterly of the air, spending almost the whole of their waking lives on the wing. Even their mating is airborne, and if you are lucky enough to see a pair during their few intense seconds of coupling it is like a glimpse of some giant black dragonfly from another age. If a swift should come down to earth – exhausted or crash-landed – it will never rise again. It's a sad irony that only when they are beached helplessly on this unfamiliar element are you able to see how exquisitely and inflexibly they are tailored for their life in the air. There can be no thrust from those stunted legs, little more than hooks for clinging to the nest and high buildings, nor lift from those narrow crescent wings. They are built for the race, not the mundane business of take-off. But it is the face that will rivet you, that alien reptilian glare with its fringed beak. To see a swift this close is an intimacy better not experienced. They belong in another element to us, in those exultant screaming flights between the houses in July, and these wheeling and tumbling, sky-high assemblies over the water as they build up the urge to migrate. It is fitting that these remote birds, one of the last to reach us in summer, are also the first to depart.

There are many other birds attracted to these sheets of water. Waders which, like the little ringed plover, winkle out insects from the muddy strips at the edge. Wagtails also feed here, and sometimes breed in the rough herbage on the banks. One nested regularly only a couple of miles from the sand martins' roundabout. The three-lane carriageway which leaves this roundabout south for London Airport runs parallel with the Colne Valley gravel pits for several miles. In places there is not much more than a hundred yards of field between the road and the water. Along one such stretch there was a long wooden fence at the inside edge of the verge, and on this fence, every last week in April, sat a cock yellow wagtail. I never got close to it, and was never able to see it for more than a few seconds. As with the martins I had to watch it through the Greenline's windows. I felt like the Railway Children watching their Old Gentleman pass in the train – only it was me that was being rushed past, not the bird, which was squatting in stoical immobility every time I saw it.

Yet we kept up our odd and formal relationship, this wagtail and I. Me, with my face pressed against London Transport glass; him perched stiffly twenty feet from the traffic, waiting (or so I liked to fancy) for the bus to pass, and looking as forlorn and adrift as an escaped canary. I have never known a bird more regular in his habits. For four consecutive years (it may yet be more: the fourth is the one I am writing in) he perched on the same twenty yards of fence for the last days of April and the first of May. I rarely glimpsed him later than this, and imagine that he then got down to the serious business of raising a family, as I once saw him with a female at the end of his long wait. I was so confident of him by the third spring that I would make a coy game out of spying him, looking at the other verge until the bus was just opposite where he should be, and then turning round. He was always there.

I would have loved to have got to know him better. Yet I suspect that if I had gone searching for him on foot he would have stayed discreetly hidden. Was it really the same bird that came back each of the four years? What was it that attracted him to this perch, only feet from the racing lorries? I never once saw him dart up after flies in the way that yellow wagtails normally love to from fences and posts. Was his patient vigil in this exposed spot a way of attracting a mate? Did they stay here, nesting in the long grass of this perilous verge when their breeding cycle began later in May?

The banks and surrounds of the pits are not the only parts which birds take advantage of. In the middle of the water there are often mounds of coarse stones and sand, left over from the washing and sifting, that form islands once the pits have been flooded. These are favourite nesting sites for our most exotic native water bird, the great crested grebe. I don't think there was one gravel pit of any size that I visited that did not have its resident pair of grebes. (Five acres is reckoned to be all the territory they need.) One pair, with great resourcefulness and tolerance I felt, had put together their reedy nest on top of one of the old car tyres which had been dumped in great numbers in one pit. The tyre they had chosen was lodged in the undergrowth near an island, and this gave it just enough stability and cover to serve as a nesting site.

They are enthralling birds to watch, whatever they are up to. I discovered this particular pair just before the eggs were due to hatch, and within a week the candy-striped chicks were on the water, scuttling and bawling after their impassive parents. For the first few weeks of their life the chicks often go for rides on one of their parent's back, whilst the other dives for food. This is no comfy treat handed out by the adult birds, but something the chicks have to work for. Great crested grebes seem to belong to the hard-knocks school of child upbringing, and time and again – especially as the chicks grew larger – I would watch a parent bird steaming out across the pit, and the young thrashing desperately behind. The race, I am sad to say, invariably went to the strongest (or at least the fastest) chicks, who would scramble thankfully aboard the parent's back – that is, except when the parent decided to be the breadwinner rather than the pram-pusher just when the leading chicks thought their leg-work had paid off. Just occasionally the whole family went down together.

It is all good slapstick to watch, though one cannot help feeling a twinge of pity for the breathless chicks. But there's no doubt that they are the winners in the long run. Within six weeks they are diving for their own fish, and after just over two months are not even moving around in a family group.

For all their hard-earned feeding and escape drill, great crested grebes were almost exterminated in this country in the middle of the last century. Their chestnut ruffs were used for ornamenting ladies' hats, and the whole skins were in great demand for muffs. One of the ways of obtaining the birds for this decadent and nasty trade involved just about the most coldly sadistic hunting game I have ever read about. This is how, with obvious relish, a distinguished nineteenth-century ornithologist described it:

A party of four shooters hire a boat with able rowers, and on a calm day, when the surface of the lake is smooth, they put off, and look out with telescopes for a large Grebe, towards which the men row; on their approach the bird dives, and the boatmen pull with vigour in the direction the bird has taken, in order to be near when it comes up to the surface to breathe. One of the shooters stations himself in the bow on the boat, one at the stern, and the others are one at each side, about the middle. At the commencement of the pursuit, when the bird is strong, it frequently comes to the surface of the water, out of shot, and has perhaps altered its course, but a good look-out is being kept by the shooters at their different posts, the bird is soon descried, and the rowers again urge the boat in chase; the bird dives again, and is again pursued, and on rising is perhaps shot at, but at too great a distance to be effectual, and the bird dives again. In this way the bird, partly exhausted by the necessity of maintaining its exertion, and perhaps slightly wounded, is unable to remain so long under water, but the boat is close at hand, the exertion must be continued, and the Grebe still rises and dives again with so much rapidity that several unsuccessful shots are frequently made. The rowers from practice can tell very nearly whenever the bird dives how many strokes of the oars will bring the boat near the place where it may be expected to rise, and by giving out this notice and counting aloud, the interest is kept up throughout the pursuit, till a fortunate shot gives the fatal blow, when the prize is handed into the boat, and the telescopes are again put into requisition to find out a new victim.

A History of British Birds,
William Yarrell, 1885

We have come on a little. Although our modern grebes, with ruffs intact, may not only look like but appear to behave like Don Quixotes, elegant but obsolete Spanish aristocrats making a last ditch stand against the tasteless backcloth of bulldozers and extraction machinery, in fact they are thriving. No chases like the one described above would be tolerated in this country now. The birds have got what they needed: water to feed in, banks and islands to nest on, and relative peace to enjoy them both.

And there is little doubt that the gravel extraction boom was largely responsible for bringing the grebe population to its present healthy level. At the height of the skin collection business, in the middle of the last century, the British population was down to about 50 pairs. The early Bird Protection Acts of 1870-1880 helped save the grebe from extinction, and censuses in the 1930s and 1940s found that there were about 1,150 breeding pairs. Yet in the next twenty years this figure went up by over 70 per cent, a figure which can be compared with the 84 per cent increase in sand and gravel production between 1948 and 1957. In several recent summers, Middlesex, with one of the most extensive gravel extraction operations in the country, has had more resident grebes than any other county. And probably half the grebes in the London area nest in flooded pits.* Yet, except in the winter, they are absent from the reservoirs and deep natural lakes. It is precisely the random contours of the gravel pits, the shallow pools, islands – and even abandoned debris – that provide the platforms the grebes need for nesting.

There's a clever little car sticker that has grown up with the inland waterways cruising craze that reads 'We Dig Canals'. Excavating them, of course, is what it does *not* mean. There have been no new canals dug in this country since competition from roads and railways made them something of a commercial anachronism. But the canal system was sufficiently important in its day to reach a total mileage of over two thousand.

---

* As I write this it has just been reported that great crested grebes have nested successfully for the first time in central London. A pair have raised two young in the Serpentine.

But as the commercial value of the canals declines, so we are beginning to realise just what an amenity these two thousand miles of navigable water represent. There are not many slow-moving, walkable, fishable rivers in our urban areas, and the canal system is consequently an asset which can't be ignored. The fish may be mediocre sport but at least you don't need thousand pound a year licences for municipal roach. And there are ready-made waterside walks in the shape of the towpaths, which can come closer to the traffic-free peace of a country lane than any other walkway in a city. Those who walk them – or boat along the adjoining water – can experience a real change of pace and perspective.

Roger Pilkington, who was perhaps more responsible than any other single person for popularising canal cruising, has caught this feeling well. It is an elemental contrast, water against metal, stillness in the midst of bustle:

> I remembered how on an April evening Fred had rowed us dreamily along part of the Regent's Canal. Overhead the buds were breaking on the elms, the rooks were cheerfully sorting themselves into pairs. My wife and I sat in the stern of the dinghy, she trailing her fingers in the water and I myself looking up dreamily at the silhouette of the trees against the evening sky, amazed that such peace and beauty could exist right there in London. Only 30 feet above us the traffic was jammed motionless on Blow-up Bridge, but it seemed to belong to another world, incredibly remote. And so it did.
>
> On the bend towards Maida Vale Fred eased off to lean out and pick up a used motor-tyre. It was a fine one, white-walled and expensive. No doubt it had once belonged to just such a smart executive saloon as those which were edging irritably along the road beyond the trees. Fred thought it would serve us as a fender, as it did through eight countries in the following years.
>
> from *Slow Boat through England*
> by Frederic Doerflinger, 1970

It's no wonder that the canals are now alive with leisure cruisers, some of them, with a thrifty resourcefulness that matches that of many of the wild inhabitants of the waterways, converted from old cargo-carrying narrow-boats. And as the yen to potter about on these placid waters spreads, so long-derelict cuts are cleared and opened up by enthusiasts. Nor have the strollers been neglected, and some local authorities – particularly in built-up areas – are tidying (or covering) up the industrial clutter that backs on to the towpaths.

But the wildlife of the canals is having a less happy time. It's benefited, to be sure, from the cleaner water, and from the simple rescue of so many arteries of life-giving water. But canals are fragile vessels, having literally to be shored-up against the stresses created by the boats and the inexorable eroding power of the water. Those responsible for the care of the canals see wildness as the enemy, choking the water and blocking the towpaths, crumbling the banks, pressing ceaselessly to turn the waterways into huge tangled ditches.

There is some cause for their fears, but not I think anything that justifies the austere and fortified condition the canals have been reduced to in many urban areas. But to understand the precarious status of the canals as living environments we must look at a little of their history and at the way they function.

Canals are by definition artificial waterways, channels cut by men along routes dictated more by economy than geology. Unlike rivers therefore, they don't always lie in water-retaining beds. Where this was the case, a vital stage in the construction of the cuts was to line the bottom and sides of the trench with 'puddle'. This was a thick paste made out of dampened and compressed clay, mixed with a little gravel or sand. It was spread 18 inches to three feet thick along the inside of the trench and allowed to dry.

Lining the canals with a material like this meant that they were able to develop a rich variety of waterweeds along their bottom and riverside flowers along their banks. Fish and insects had an abundance of food, and birds moved in to feed off both. So, for a while the canals were as rich with wildlife as any slow-moving river.

But the use of puddle has its drawbacks. Unlike the sterile concrete often used to line reservoirs, it is not impervious to water. There is a continuous leakage through it, which combined with evaporation from the surface and loss of water through the locks, means that the canals have continually to be topped up from reservoirs especially constructed for this purpose.

But more serious than actual leakage is the gradual wearing away of the puddle and of the banks behind it. Erosion is seldom a serious problem with rivers. Most have already worn their way through to harder rocks and soils, and are only eating into these imperceptibly. The fine silt that is formed by this process is flushed away to the sea by the current.

But in a canal the water may only have to eat away a couple of feet of clay before striking softer soil. What eroding power it lacks from the absence of a regular current it gains from the wash of the boats. This is no new problem (as it is in the Norfolk Broads, for instance, because of the growing flotillas of motor cruisers). It has existed just as long as wide and heavy boats have moved along these narrow channels. From their earliest introduction in the latter half of the eighteenth century, the horse-drawn boats moved at between 3 and 4 m.p.h. – almost exactly the speed at which most pleasure cruisers are advised to move today. Yet even the marginal increase in speed which was brought about by the use of mules on some runs, had an alarming effect upon the boats' wash, as one writer observed in 1805:

> We observed a constant elevation of the water before the
> passage boat, as it moved along, of at least 9 inches, and
> perhaps more than a foot at times; and the rapidity with
> which the water ran backwards, between the boat and
> the side of the canal, appeared to have a most destructive

effect upon the latter, particularly on the towing path side; and often this was laid quite under water, for considerable distances together, by the surge or wave opposite to the head of the boat as it passed along; while the labour of towing was most materially increased.

The Canal Age, Charles Hadfield, 1968

In a moving stream this would be the end of it. The particles of earth would be carried away by the same action that dislodged them. But in a canal they simply settle again on the bottom. This is not to say that the water in a canal is absolutely stationary. Every time a lock is emptied something like 50,000 gallons of water are shunted one further stage downstream. But when you compare this figure with the one million gallons per day passed by a stream 2 inches deep, 2 feet wide and flowing at 4 m.p.h. (a canal might be 6 feet deep and 20 feet wide) you realise what a paltry cleansing action the sluicing of the locks provides. And as if this wasn't enough, the silt settling on the bottom helps feed the waterweeds, which may already be running amok from the build-up of nitrate fertilisers in the water (washed off from fields and diluted only slowly in these sluggish waters). An un-tended canal will be choked with mud and weed after very few years.

The boats play a double-edged role in all this. Although they are the major cause of bank erosion and the consequent silting-up of the channels, they also help to scour them, breaking up the weed and keeping the silt mobile with their wash. And since more boats mean more opening of locks, they indirectly disperse their own litter.

It's a nightmarishly complex web of forces for anyone trying to work out a management policy. Canals are really little more than long, thin ponds, yet they're treated as – and expected to behave like – rivers. And their commercial roots can't be ignored. They must be kept serviceable for the pleasure boats that use them now and the commercial traffic that may one day build up in them again.

British Waterways' attack on the problems has always been hampered by the paltry budget they are allowed. In an effort to cut costs they have devised a technique for carrying out two of the maintenance tasks in one operation. Where the erosion of the banks is serious they shore them up with concrete and metal palings. At the same time they dredge the bottom of surplus mud and gravel and use it to level off the surface of the path, smothering the flowers beneath. Where the dredgings are largely gravel it can be years before many new plants can get a roothold, and for that time a towpath stroll can be an uncomfortable, noisy and lifeless experience. It's not much better when they are largely mud, for the turfless path can become a dangerous mire in winter. I've seen this happening even in the heart of a National Park in the Brecon Beacons in Wales. The Brecon Canal must be one of the most beautiful waterways, natural or man-made, in the whole British Isles. In some stretches it actually skirts, at an altitude of 300 feet, the side of the mountains. The towpath is clothed with flowers in the late spring: sweeps of white wild garlic and sweet woodruff falling to the very edge of the water in the hanging beech woods; lady's smock, violets, lousewort and water mint along the damper parts of the path. Yet in some summers I have watched dredged silt being indiscriminately dumped for hundreds of yards along the outer edge of this towpath. It will be years before the old bankside flowers can beat back the nettles and the docks.

There is no doubt that the Brecon Canal does need periodic dredging. It has a narrow and shallow channel, and the increasing number of boats which use it tear more soil off the banks than they carry down with them through the locks. Yet by taking this silt away (and maybe selling it as fertiliser to cover the transport costs) the canal could be kept a delight to walk beside as well as to boat on.

In urban areas the towpath flowers not only suffer incidentally in the same way but are systematically destroyed every spring by weedkiller sprays. British Waterways are understandably anxious that the paths don't become overgrown, particularly in areas like lock surrounds where there has to be a deal of nimble footwork. But it's questionable whether this should be the rule for the main stretches of towpath. A glance at a few rural footpaths will show that human use tends to keep a path in a condition appropriate to the amount it's used. If many feet are tramping it every day it is kept flat and open; if it is the more secret and personal route of a few hardy ramblers then it stays wilder and more overgrown – which is how they would wish it.

Yet although it is now almost exclusively walkers who use the towpaths (their original purpose was to provide a route for the horses that towed the boats), British Waterways insist that they should be kept in 'good order' and that in aesthetic terms, the appearance of a weedless towing path is preferable to one which is ragged and overgrown. But it would be a shame if by weeds they meant all wild flowers. I cannot believe that in towns of all places, where wild greenery and colour is so precious, the public prefer to walk amongst the grotesque, scorched remnants of nettles and thistles than among buttercups and wild mint. For that is the choice. The rank and often untidy plants that are unpopular with public and Waterways Board alike (although not without their own brand of rough charm, as I suggested earlier), are not the natural flora of the canal banks. They are the direct result of the rough handling of the soil in these places. As in a new road verge or any other disturbed ground, it is the tallest, most prolific and fastest growing plants that are the first to be established. Only under a gentle and regular programme of mowing can their seed production be cut down, light let in, and the more dainty herbs be given a chance.

British Waterways have caught themselves in a vicious circle. Weeds flourish in the disturbed soil and total weedkiller is called in to knock them out. Bare soil is created again – and an ideal habitat for the rough plants to colonise again the following year. (I have been saddened to see that the anglers, normally vigilant guardians of the biological health of the canals, have begun collaborating in this process. A fad has grown up for personalised aerosol weedkiller sprays, carried in the hamper and used to exterminate any plants which might conceivably ensnare a cack-handed cast, or disturb the comfort of a reclining seat.)

In rural areas the Waterways Board run a sensitive mowing programme (where its benefits are not cancelled out by sludge dumping) even on quite narrow towpaths. It ought to be just as possible to return to mowing on the considerably broader urban paths, and build up a rich sward that is both pleasant and safe to walk on.

There is a stretch of canal I often visit that sums up in less than 400 yards most of the problems and opportunities I have been talking about. It lies in one of those areas at the edge of a town where all the service facilities seem to cluster together, preying off each other like some complex technological food web. At this point the cut runs through the centre of a rectangular strip of land not much more than 300 yards wide, bounded at one edge by a railway line and the other by an arterial road. Between them a sewage filtration works, draining its semi-purified water into the canal; a watercress bed, fed by a small stream linked with the canal; a thin strip of arable land, and a refuse dump filling up the wasted land between railway and water. Overhead loop huge skeins of electricity cables and under the ground, the North Sea gas pipes. They all lie as tightly bunched as wires in a conduit.

I visited this stretch at the tail-end of the spring. It was a warm overcast afternoon in mid-June, and the midges were drifting in clouds over the water. There was not much to be seen as I walked out of the town. The sprayers had been there a few weeks before me, and what vegetation there was left along the towpath bank was a tangle of litter as burnt and bent as if it had been attacked by a flame-thrower. There were no weed seeds for the finches, nor flowers for the butterflies.

But as I came in sight of the stretch I described above, I could see that the air above the canal was alive with birds. Every house martin within a mile's radius that wasn't actually sitting on eggs must have been gathered there. The bulk of the birds – and there were over a hundred of them – were hawking for flies over the sewage filtration beds. Some had even joined the starlings taking roundabout rides on the sprinklers. The remainder were taking it in turns to make strafing runs down the canal, or were resting up in short ranks on the telegraph wires. It was a real festival of martins, a celebration perhaps of a fresh hatch of midges, ripe for the harvest.

They are infectiously joyful, these gatherings of hirundines. I know of no other types of bird which go about their communal flights with such dash and relish. Migrating flocks of geese and soaring hawks may be more dramatic, but for sheer exuberance there is nothing to beat the martins and swallows and swifts. They feed like madcap trapezists, racing and tumbling past each other, yet staying as smoothly packed as if they were performing in a circus tent.

I had been watching the martins for some time when I saw an unexpectedly long wagtail loop over the canal towards the watercress beds. There were plenty of brisk pied wagtails around, and I had spied one yellow wagtail in the mud at the edge of the beds. But this was neither of these species, and even in silhouette looked unmistakably like a grey to me. Now although it wasn't impossible that a stray bird had stayed over from the winter, grey wagtails are really birds of the fast hill streams of the North and West, and nest only rarely in the Home Counties. They move South and East in the winter to lowland cress beds and sewage farms, and are normally gone again by the end of March. But I watched this wagtail pitch down in the watercress and there was no doubt that it was a female grey. It was an exquisitely graceful bird, with a flighty tail as long again as its head and body, ash grey back and yellow underparts. After a few dainty rushes for insects it flew on to the towpath about twenty yards in front of me. Through my binoculars I could see that there was another smaller wagtail crouched amongst some stones on the path. Any doubts I had that it was a juvenile grey vanished when the adult female stuffed a sheaf of leggy insects into its beak.

It was a spine-tingling moment. As far as I knew grey wagtails hadn't bred in this area for over twenty years, when there were still trout in the stream, horses on the towpath and swimmers in the canal. It was heartening and not a little surprising that they had returned at a time when this little patch of wetland seemed to be in a state of siege.

So with the air above me full of exultant martins, and this scarce and prodigal bird in front of me, come back to breed in the parish, I was hardly in a state of mind to cope with what happened next. The juvenile wagtail, which had scarcely moved a feather whilst it was being fed, suddenly seemed to collapse. Its legs buckled and it sank awkwardly down on to its breast. Its head arched slowly and corkscrewed round until it was almost facing backwards. With one wing stretched out on the ground and the other threshing the air it finally flipped over on its side. I thought at first that it was dust-bathing or drying out some damp feathers. But these shudders were no toilet routine. They reminded me all too sickeningly of the terrible, incoherent nervous spasms of birds I had seen poisoned by organo-chlorine pesticides.

I don't know what I imagined I could do, but I ran feebly towards the fledgling, and it jumped up and flew low and steadily another ten yards up the towpath. Almost immediately it fell over on its side again, and tried to writhe forwards as if its legs had been tied. By this time its mother had returned and started to dither round her infant, her mouth bristling with food. Whatever was wrong with the young bird, it had not affected its appetite. For a while the mother bird attended almost abjectly upon her youngster, hovering a few feet from him, darting this way and that for single flies which she instantly dashed into his beak. Then the fledgling would stumble or fly a few more feet.

I suppose I watched them like this for twenty minutes. It was like some grotesque *pas de deux* mocking physical affliction: the mother bird with her exquisite, gushing grace fluttering around the head of her fledgling; him, hunched on the ground twitching and groping to pull his movements together into some order that fitted with hers. Happily he seemed to improve towards the end of this time. I began to hope, no doubt against all scientific reason, that, like us, young birds had growing pains, or touches of the rheumatics in dank weather. Perhaps he was simply sick. I shall never know. The one piece of evidence I had was that for the first time the banks of the watercress beds had been sprayed along with the towpath, and it was in one of these that the grey wagtails had quite likely built their nest. Although most weed killers are supposed to break down days and sometimes even hours after they have been applied, very little work has been done on their effects on higher forms of life. But we do know that Paraquat, one of the most widely used sprays, is a deadly poison to man. One mouthful of the undiluted substance, even if spat out immediately, is fatal. Between 1967 and 1970, 24 people died from Paraquat poisoning. In 1970 all the six cases of 'accidental death from pesticides and fertilisers' were caused by Paraquat. The world total of deaths is over 60.

All this from a substance that has a reputation for being harmless to animals and being ecologically 'clean'. Would a faceful of a herbicide as lethal as this – however diluted – really have no effect on a chick a few days old? To judge by the size of this fledgling it would have hatched at just about the time of spraying.

The margin by which wildlife hangs on in areas such as these is so precarious that I don't think it's unreasonable to fear the worst. Here the dividing line was drawn, symbolically narrow, by the canal itself. Just thirty feet of water separated near sterility from abundance. On my side was the wide towpath, concreted at the edge and covered with a thick layer of gravel. On the other, a bank as green and craggy as any natural streamside. Hawthorns and willows drooped into the water and moorhens hid out in the tangled maze of their roots and branches. The grassy slopes between were thick with the young shoots of angelica, great willowherb and meadowsweet. They weren't in flower yet, nor were some of the smaller plants I could see through my binoculars. They were, encouragingly, a collection of some of the native riverside flowers of the old herbalists. There was marsh woundwort, a modestly elegant member of the nettle family, which John Gerard used, apparently successfully, to cure a Holborn shoemaker stabbed in the throat: 'a most mortall wound . . . in such sort, that when I gave him drinke it came forth at the wound, which likewise did blowe out a candle.' Next to it was gipsywort, of which the seventeenth-century botanist Caleb Threlkeld had this to say: 'Some call this the Gipsy-herb, because those stroling cheats called Gipsies do dye themselves of a blackish Hue with the Juice of this Plant, the better to pass for *Africans* by their tanned looks, and swarthy Hides, to babble the credulous and ignorant by the Practice of Magick and Fortune-telling; they being indeed a nasty Sink of all Nations, living by Rapine, Filching, Pilfering and Imposture.' (Gipsywort does indeed give a fast dark dye, though it's hard to believe that gipsies felt they could improve their precarious social status by blacking themselves up!)

And amongst them all were a few stems of water figwort, with its strange globular purple flowers. Children in the West Country call this plant crowdy-kit and fiddlestrings, from the squeaking noises they make by bowing one stalk across another. The sounds come from the vibrations in the parchment-like wings stretched along each edge of the square stems. I tried out some crowdying myself later in the year, with some stalks which had been knocked down on a disused canal nearby. I got the violin-lesson whine all right, but my instrument was in tatters after thirty seconds' furious bowing!

But even on the stony towpath there were a few plants which, growing near the very edge or sprouting late, had escaped the weedkiller: redleg, fool's watercress, water plantain. A few more, with that resilience and adaptability that we see time and again in nature, actually seemed to find the spartan conditions of life along a modern canal to their liking. So, dedicated to their tolerance, I give this short roll of honour of those plants that have come through.

Lunularia cruciata

There is no English name for this diminutive liverwort, which I found only inches above the water, anchored to some stone towpath supports. It smelt slightly of cucumber, and looked as scaly as an armadillo's skin. One of the characteristic features of this group of non-flowering plants is just this plating of the unribbed leaves. In most cases there are three rows of leaves along each stem, those in one row being smaller (or occasionally missing altogether), and lying under the other rows. Liverworts are very happy on stone, for they don't have true roots, but a net of fine white hairs, called rhizoids, which grow out of the undersides of the leaves and clamp them to hard surfaces.

The other condition in which liverworts revel is damp, so it's easy to see why this stone bank overhanging the cut was colonised. (*Lunularia* is also probably one of our few non-flowering weeds, being rarely found far from human constructions, and may have been brought over to this country from the Mediterranean in Roman times.) They are ancient plants, having evolved far earlier than flowers and needing water as a carrier for their reproductive cells.

Each liverwort leaf carries both male and female organs. In the spring, if the plant is sufficiently damp, the male vessel swells and bursts, and the reproductive cells are liberated. Again, given enough damp, these can start swimming about on the surface of the plant. They are conveniently very fatty by nature and float to the surface of any film of water.

The presence of moisture is crucial right through the process, and it's also responsible for opening the female vessel to receive the free-swimming sperm.

If fertilisation is successful by June, spores will start to develop inside the female vessel and will be liberated the following spring, each one, with luck, growing into a new plant.

Orange balsam

This flower had the privilege of being first discovered in the wild by the philosopher John Stuart Mill, in 1822. It was brought over here from its native America some time before that as a garden flower. It's made a delightful addition to our flora with its nasturtium-like flowers, orange bells flecked inside with reddish-brown, and we should be glad that it found a way out of those nineteenth-century gardens. But how did it spread from that first natural site on the banks of a Surrey river to perch on one of the few earthy patches along this towpath?

The answer lies in the seeds. The ripe seed pods of all the members of the balsam family have the singular habit of exploding petulantly when touched, and throwing their fruits as much as six feet away. Hence the Latin name for the family, *impatiens*. The seeds of the orange balsam have the extra advantage of being light and corky enough to float on water. So once it had escaped from the garden to a waterside, the plant was poised for colonisation. Launched into the water, the seeds floated off like tiny coracles, dispersing themselves through the waterway system, until they lodged in a bank. Where there was no way through by water, birds and anglers and boatmen no doubt inadvertently helped them on their way. The canal system has always been a popular haunt of the plant, maybe because the slowness of the current gives the seeds a better chance of making a beachhead.

Guelder rose

I must confess that when I found my first guelder rose bush, growing opposite the sewage farm along this stretch of canal, I thought I'd stumbled across a wild redcurrant. It was in the early autumn and to my youthful and indiscriminate eye the clusters of bright red berries and lobed leaves looked very curranty. There could have been no confusion a month or so later, when the leaves had turned a brilliant scarlet and the berries become heavy and waxy. Nor would there have been if I had discovered it coming into flower as it was that June afternoon. Guelder rose has perhaps the most startlingly beautiful blossoms of all our flowering shrubs. The flower heads are made up from a cluster of small creamy blooms encircled as meticulously and tidily as a posy by a necklace of large china-white, five-petalled flowers. It is an untypical piece of excess, for these showy outer flowers are quite sterile, and it is the diminutive inner blooms that produce the glossy red berries. Guelder rose flowers have a tantalising scent: spicy, damp, a little reminiscent of moss. Geoffrey Grigson likens them to 'crisply fried, well-peppered trout'.

The shrub loves damp places (indeed it does actually grow with redcurrant in the Fens) and the building of the canals opened up whole new habitats for it. It was surviving well on this towpath, laid well back from the centre of the path, just beyond the spray-gun's reach.

Horsetail

The horsetails are the last surviving members of a family of plants that flourished in the Carboniferous period, something like 300 million years ago. You would expect a plant with that sort of ancestry to have some formidable techniques for survival, and it is not really surprising to find that horsetails are barely bruised by most weedkillers. Except in size they have scarcely changed at all from those huge feathery trees – more like bottle-brushes, really, than horses' tails – whose rotting remains helped build up our coal deposits.

That June day there were just a few young shoots poking through the gravel. Each one was no more than two or three inches high, a stiff jointed central stem carrying ruffs of hair-like bristles. It looks a simple enough plant, yet its rather austere form hides a fascinating and complex life history. Under the surface of a horsetail colony is a complex web of roots, sometimes extending many feet down into the ground. These roots carry knobbly tubers, and if any one of these is dislodged or broken off it can develop into a new plant. In March and April the root system sends up its reproductive shoots, which look a little like brown asparagus spears. The bulb at the top of these shoots produce clouds of spores, some of which develop into 'male' plants and others into females. In the right damp conditions – for which a canal bank is ideal – cells from the male plants can swim and fertilise cells on the surface of the females. When this happens successfully another individual horsetail is produced. If it does not, the main root system still sends up its brushy green shoots later in the year. By the autumn these have become wiry and tough, and there was a time when they were used for scouring pots, pans, wooden utensils and pewter. One of its old names was pewter-wort.

Coltsfoot

All that was left of the coltsfoot plants along this bank were some patches of the hoof-shaped leaves (somewhat singed at the edges) which were responsible for the plant's name. Coltsfoot is one of those plants in which the blooms appear before the leaves, sometimes as early as the middle of February. They are a perfect flower for these clear, late winter days; sharp yellow buttons standing out against the brown earth, uncluttered by leaves or new herbage. Coltsfoot seems to have a liking for fairly bare soil (particularly in moist areas) where there has been disturbance two or three years previously, as in a recently made-up towpath.

The fruits are like small over-ripe bananas, and carry at their end a parachute of downy hairs much longer than the seed itself, so that they can be easily carried away on the wind. They're usually off and away before the spraying; but in any case the root system of coltsfoot, whose growth plays as great a role in the spread of coltsfoot as the seeds, is very tough and not much affected by most weedkillers.

ginger
blue grey
black

light green centre
reseda
emerald
black

charcoal
charcoal

ginger
peach
apricot

body
seeming
pink

yellow ochr
light reflection

black
paynes grey
thorax

triangular
thorax

ginger → apricot

PART TWO

Summer: Living Together

Pests, pets and predators

IT WAS LATE JUNE and I was driving along an A road just west of London, when they seemed to loom up in the road in front of me. It was a scene that I'd jokingly conjured up in my mind many times before, whenever I'd seen one of those ominous road signs HEAVY PLANT CROSSING.

Imagine, if you can, a typical suburban carriageway, running between lines of thirties-style factories done-up like cinemas with vaulted entrances and plaster cake decorations; down its edges, wide pavements, smart fences and bus stops. A place to go about your business in, built for the respectable passage of people and trade. And there, in a forty-yard stretch of land left over between two of the factories, this jungle of appalling plants, eight, nine feet tall some of them, bursting through the railings on to the pavement, drooping their eighteen-inch-wide flower-heads over the very heads of the passers-by.

It was giant hogweed, Britain's most notorious plant. Never before had I seen it in such profusion, or pressing so rampantly close to the polite and orderly life of the suburbs. For once a plant's Latin name has caught its character far better than any traditional English tag. I can't think of a more appropriate or memorable name for the plant than *Heracleum mantegazzianum*, with its dedication to Hercules and sinister buzz in the tail.

Up until 1970, few people besides botanists and some eccentric horticulturalists knew much about this plant. It had been introduced from the Caucasus in 1893 as an exotic curiosity for Victorian gardens. But it was too gawky and downright disturbing for most tastes, and soon drifted out of fashion. Occasionally a dormant seed

77

would spring to life in a garden. But who knew what it was? A giant angelica? A freak cow parsley? Then in 1970, an increasing number of cases of children with persistent and inexplicable rashes on their lips and hands led doctors back to this plant. Children, no doubt fascinated by giant hogweeds' unearthly appearance, couldn't keep their hands off it, and had been making pea-shooters from its stems.

The secret was out, and the Press had a field day. Triffids were no science fiction fantasy. They were loose in our own land. They had escaped from those garden-corner enclosures and spread along any piece of damp waste ground they could find: canals in Wales, river banks in the lowlands of Scotland, and patches of low-lying marshland around our cities. Every part of the plant, alive or dead, contained irritant chemicals that could cause severe and long-lasting rashes if they penetrated too deep into a sensitive skin. The plant was dubbed a public menace, and encouraged by the Press, vigilantes went out to wage war on it. Plants were cut down, dug up, sprayed and burnt. Six-column photos appeared in the papers to help the public recognise the beast. But it was little use. *Mantegazzianum* was indifferent to weedkillers and had a root system that would defy an excavating machine. It continued its insidious expansion along veins of damp ground.

Still, I had never seen such a blatant plantation as this one laid out between factory and pavement like a Parks and Gardens chrysanthemum bed, and it seemed worth breaking the parking laws for a closer look. Giant hogweed is a plant you would feel a certain respect for even if you weren't aware of its reputation. The hairy stem is as thick as a small tree-trunk at the base, and blotched with purple; the leaves are huge and jagged.

From the pavement I could see that the plants covered an area about forty yards square. In the centre of the square was a damp hollow, or maybe a small stream, and the ground sloped gently down towards this. Contoured like this the hogweeds looked magnificent, and I have a feeling that the architects of those Hollywood-style factories would have approved of this uncommissioned touch of macabre extravagance – vegetable piranhas in the swimming pool.

Late in 1970, I came across a case not unlike the hogweed scare. I was coming home on the train one night, and for want of something better to read picked up a copy of British Rail's *Rail News* that had been abandoned on the carriage floor. On the news page was this report:

> Hard on the heels of the giant hogweed reported in August *Rail News*, comes another rare and dangerous plant – the thorn-apple.
>
> It was spotted at New Milton station by retired chemist and local botanist, Bernard Hannan. He told his next-door neighbour, Llewelyn Trudgeon, one of Waterloo's assistants.
>
> The thorn-apple has a strong smell and its flowers are either purple or white. The nasty-looking seed pod is like a horse chestnut with spikes.
>
> Mr Trudgeon was told by his botanist friend that the plant was poisonous and contained drugs which produced hallucinations and dilating pupils of the eyes.
>
> 'It is very rare and was last recorded in this country in 1962,' he added.
>
> Apparently the drug stramonium, which came from the plant, was once used for the alleviation of asthma. And it is believed wizards in medieval times used it.
>
> New Milton SM Desmond Mantle was told that the plant was in his station car park and arranged for it to be destroyed.
>
> After hacking down the 3 ft plant they dug up its roots and burned the lot.
>
> *Rail News*, October 1970

Happily, this wasn't the only thorn-apple left in our island. It pops up every year in waste ground all over the south of England.

But it is sad that such a beautiful and fascinating plant should be so maliciously and ignorantly destroyed, just as the 'wizards' who reputedly once used it were. (If they did they certainly weren't medieval ones here: the plant wasn't introduced to this country until the end of the sixteenth century.) Certainly all parts of the plant are deadly poisonous, if taken in sufficient quantities. Certainly children have been attracted by its conkery fruits – though their formidable spines and nauseous smell must deter all but the most adventurous. But I wonder if this is sufficient to justify destroying thorn-apple on sight? Stramonium extracted from the leaves and flowers of the plant still has an honourable place in conventional medicine and thorn-apple to provide it is still grown commercially in this country. Maybe inside the drug firms' farms is where it should be confined. But its natural history is part of our social history, in the same way as that of better known introductions like the corn poppy. To subject it to a kind of biological censorship because it is dangerous is to my mind as questionable as the burning of books because they are unsettling.

What, then, are thorn-apple's credentials, that might justify it being offered a little more respect? It was originally a native of Peru, and it was John Gerard who first grew it in this country, in his garden in Holborn. So delighted was he by its showy trumpet flowers that he 'dispersed (it) through this land' – as well as having fun with it in his 'surgery':

> The juice of Thorn-apples boiled with hogs grease to
> the form of an unguent or salve, cures all inflammations
> whatsoever, all manner of burnings or scaldings, as well of
> fire, water, boiling lead, gun-pouder, as that which comes by
> lightning, and that in very short time, as my selfe have found
> by my daily practise, to my great credit and profit. The first
> experience came from Colchester, where Mistress Lobel
> a merchant's wife there being most grievously burned by
> lightning, and not finding ease or cure in any other thing, by

this found helpe and was perfectly cured when all hope was past, by the report of Mr William Ram publique Notarie of the said towne.

The Herball, 1597

A hundred years later another herbalist, John Pechey, reported in his *Compleat Herbal of Physical Plants* that the powdered seeds were slipped by thieves into their intended victims' beer, to drive them temporarily mad. 'And Wenches give half a dram of it to their Lovers, in beer or wine. Some are so well skill'd in dosing of it, that they can make men mad for as many hours as they please.'

Rum goings-on indeed, that today would upset more than station-masters. But thorn-apple soon acquired a more respectable role. It was found to be invaluable in the treatment of all sorts of respiratory disorders, particularly asthma. Its potency is due to narcotic drugs like atropine and hyoscine that sedate the nerve endings. Although it is grown commercially in this country, the bulk of our supplies have always come from Eastern Europe. So supplies were badly hit in the last war, during the blockade of Britain. The authorities were thankful then for the odd wild specimens, and the County Herb Committees were asked to gather their leaves and flowers to augment the stepped-up production from our own farms.

Seeds that have escaped from the commercial farms probably account for many of the specimens that occur in the wild today. Others arrive as impurities in bags of South American fertiliser. But they could equally be relics from the days when thorn-apple was grown much more widely in this country. The 500 or so seeds which are scattered when the spiny pod explodes have been proved to stay fertile for exceptionally long periods. In Anglesey, for instance, when some old land near Maes-y-Porth was put under the plough for the first time for well over a hundred years, there were thorn-apples up in a matter of months.

One last trick. Take a few of the prickly 'apples' and soak them in surgical spirit. If you then shine a light through the infusion, it radiates a soft green fluorescence.

When you unearth a pedigree like this for a plant it's not so easy to condemn it. It's true that destroying a plant is not quite the same as knocking down a historic building; unless it's on the verge of extinction (which is not impossible) there are always duplicates somewhere or seeds lying in wait. But like buildings, plants have contexts. They never grow completely at random. There is always a story behind their persistence in one place and their sudden arrival in another. And dried-up museum specimens and textbook illustrations just can't capture the force of these stories like the living plant, growing where it belongs. So much is lost: the sheer malignant bulk of the giant hogweed; the ironies in the contrast between thorn-apple's elegant swan-necked flowers and its potent chemistry (would you believe it's a member of the same family as the potato and tomato?). And what inescapable physical evidence of the resilience of seeds that field in Anglesey must have given, covered suddenly with a rash of strange plants that had been seen there in no living person's memory!

I remember the excitement I felt when I found two plants that summer, sprawling venomously and quite unexpectedly in the same patch of hemlock-covered waste ground I had visited in the spring. Their seeds too must have been biding their time under the soil for decades.

Yet giant hogweed and thorn-apple are undeniably dangerous. The fact that they have a taste for human territory simply makes them more so. But it ought also to make deciding what to do about them more difficult. For it's just that sense that life can go on with a different set of priorities to our own that makes the persistence of wildlife in urban areas so valuable.

Even if it were desirable to wipe out a whole species from an area, it is virtually impossible. Isolated plants, fragments of root and seeds will nearly always persist and maybe make the plant doubly dangerous to the curious precisely by increasing its rarity. The only real solution is to get to know the plant. British Rail could have done their bit for the thorn-apple. Instead of exterminating that car park specimen they could have rigged up a small fence around it and added an explanatory label. It would hardly have been a more expensive job than the excavation they mounted.

Summer is the real testing time for the willingness of man and the natural world to live together. Animal populations are at their highest, fruit trees and vegetable patches are being scrumped by hungry juvenile birds, and most plants are invitingly in flower and occupying more human territory than at any other time of the year.

Poisonous plants are perhaps the most extreme examples of that category of wild creatures called 'pests' whose luxuriant growth at this time makes them decidedly unpopular. It's an ill-defined group, changing with fashion, season and location. And there are many creatures that never find their way into it. There can be very few people, for instance, who feel anything but affection for robins and bluebells (though if bluebells had feelings I doubt whether they'd say this was mutual). But the majority of living organisms, from the mosses that upset the velvet uniformity of a lawn to the deer that occasionally take a snack in the allotments, have made an enemy somewhere, some time. The problem – particularly acute in urban areas with their dense populations of humans – is that one man's pest is another man's pet.

In the working countryside the problem is at least more clear-cut, if no less vexing. If chickens are being eaten or cattle poisoned, then the conflict is one between food and amenity. Both, in different ways, are crucial to our well-being. But what are the issues in a town? An occasional noise, a little inconvenience, some fouling of the buildings? They are hardly matters of life and death and certainly not the prerogatives of the natural inhabitants of urban areas. Giant hogweeds haven't yet gone on to the offensive and started mugging pedestrians. Carrion crows don't break into Smithfield meat market or bindweeds tear down buildings. It is a matter of how much slight discomfort we are prepared to tolerate in some of our urban affairs for the chance to experience a little wildness in others.

Take the town pigeon. It's typical of our muddled attitudes towards urban wildlife that tens of thousands of these are lovingly fed every lunchtime, whilst in the early mornings, before the bird-fanciers are about, the borough pest controllers go after them with amplified alarm calls, poisoned grain and wobbly perches.

The problem with pigeons is their droppings. On buildings where pigeons roost in large numbers these can build up layers a foot or more thick. Bird droppings are corrosive to stonework, and old limestone statues and carving-work are especially vulnerable. They can also transmit diseases like psittacosis to humans (though no cases of any disease have ever been traced back to wild bird droppings in this country, and overseas they are almost exclusively confined to the public health workers employed to clean up droppings). But there would be no problem at all if it weren't for the huge numbers of pigeons that live exclusively in towns and cities (there are something like 20,000 pairs in the ten square miles of central London alone). And there would not be such numbers if the pigeons hadn't adapted so inventively to town life.

You have only to look at the jumble of sizes and colours – stretching from dirty grey through cinnamon to pure white – in a gathering of town (or feral) pigeons to appreciate that they have a real mongrel ancestry. The original of the feral pigeon was the wild rock dove, and the double black wing-bars and white rump of that species can still be seen in many of their urban descendants. Rock doves probably arrived in cities via medieval dovecotes. Finding the tall buildings not unlike their original cliffside habitats, they stayed and interbred with other escaped birds from domestic pigeon lofts and later with the numerous strains which have been developed for racing.

There is always a place for a vegetarian scavenger in a modern city, and feral pigeons have filled this role more effectively than any other bird. So flexible are they as a species that what they eat depends almost wholly on where they live. Those in dockland areas feast off spillage from grain shipments. They are real opportunists, swooping down on to lorries carrying bags of grain if there is any sign that some has been spilled. They've even been seen riding on the conveyer belts that carry grain from ship to silo – an unhappy journey for some of the birds, whose obsessive foraging makes them forget to hop off in time.*

In town centres feral pigeons will eat anywhere. They forage in the gutters, take weed seeds from wasteland, strut about the permanent way in main-line stations after carriage sweepings, and loiter in open-air restaurants like pickpockets, ready to snatch scraps of food off the very plates of the diners. With such sharp wits and enterprise the town pigeon couldn't fail.

I once tracked a small band of pigeons around on their paradings. Although I knew that these birds might never have walked on grass or earth, I was still mystified by how they could find anything to eat on what looked like bare concrete to me. Yet on they would strut in that blissful mixture of sex and food which makes up most of a pigeon's life, seizing morsels which had previously been quite invisible to me, pausing now and then for a little amorous chest-puffing, which would then slide so smoothly into another food-sampling run that it looked like a table mannerism.

I soon found that a pigeon would drop whatever it was trying to eat if I chased it noisily enough. I could then move in to examine the

---

* There are reports from time to time of pigeons commuting purposefully about London on the tube, striding on at one station and leaving at the next.

left-overs. It was a rather heartless experiment but it showed what a discriminating and economical beachcomber the town pigeon is. Not once did I catch a bird trying anything completely inedible. One gave a piece of dried-out orange peel a few shakes, and a small gang were demolishing the more juicy and caked-up corners of a fish and chip bag. A few also seemed to be downing tiny stones for their gizzards. But not one bird went for the spent matches, beer-can rings or plain, unflavoured newspaper scraps that were just as plentiful. Birds have a poorly developed sense of smell, so these pigeons had almost certainly learned to recognise and select by appearance a whole range of non-natural but edible products. Some of the snacks dropped by the birds scuttling before me were at first sight scarcely recognisable as food. There were tiny fragments of potato crisp, squashed raisins, peanuts, and pieces of bread flattened by human feet, covered with dirt and baked by the sun to the consistency of cardboard. But the pigeons had rumbled their food value. They worried away at the larger bits, shaking them in their beaks until a piece broke off and shifted into position in which it could be swallowed in one.

In city centres of course, fresh food (usually bread or grain) is fed directly to pigeons by kindly humans, the plump whites, as ever, getting more of a share than the poor blacks.

But it's those scrawny dark pigeons which have the last laugh. An increase in the dark pigment melanin in the tissues helps many creatures to survive in industrial areas, by making them less conspicuous against grimy surfaces. Black animals can also absorb more heat energy from their surroundings.

But for melanistic pigeons the chief advantage seems to be that they are able to breed for virtually the whole year. Most wild rock doves stop breeding between November and January, and in natural surroundings this spell of inactivity, sparked off hormonally when the amount of daylight falls below a certain level, serves as a check against breeding when food supplies are short. But this is not only unnecessary but may be even a disadvantage in towns, where, thanks to man, there is likely to be as much food around in winter as in the summer. The dark pigeons, genetically able to breed throughout the year, can take maximum advantage of the food that is available for feeding their young, and raise numbers of full broods as a result.

It is extraordinary that this one variation in pigmentation should bring in its wake so many other bonuses for a city bird. As a mournful official in South London remarked, retreating from his fifth unsuccessful attempt to drive feral pigeons out of his manor: 'These pigeons are not like the ones people keep in their back gardens and which are really quite attractive. These urban dwellers are a breed of drab looking characters which just make a mess on the pavement.' The ratepayers, to judge from their food parcels, would disagree. It's a question, in the end, of how much inconvenience you are prepared to put up with for the sake of this close contact with some marginally wild creatures.

It's the same with the grey squirrels which haunt, with such dash and style, so many town parks and suburban gardens. On the credit side is an attractive and appealing mammal, a performer of astonishing acrobatic tricks, that will rest on your shoulder, feed from your hand, yet still keep the suspicious, alien eye of a true wild animal. On the debit side, a raider of birds' nests and destroyer of young trees.

I must confess to a thoroughly sentimental affection for urban grey squirrels. In the countryside these animals are devastating young beech and conifer plantations, and they probably need to be controlled. But they are not the same menace inside towns, and I can forgive them almost any depredations for their daredevil stunts and enterprise.

There have been reports of them burgling bread from the window ledges of tower blocks as much as sixteen storeys up. And I have seen them myself tightroping along washing lines after tits' nut baskets. For sheer brazen audacity though, the one I watched in the heart of the Botanical Garden at Oxford, sniffing about the lawns and rooting up colchicum bulbs, wins the prize. At those other famous gardens at Kew they add insult to injury by chewing the meticulously inscribed botanical labels as well as the plants!

It's understandable, given the thousands of young shrubs planted in places like Regent's Park every year, that the keepers feel they have to control the squirrels' numbers. (No doubt this also is done in the secrecy of the early mornings.) But it's an unfair piece of propagandising that other naturalists should have christened the grey squirrel the 'tree rat'. Both rats and squirrels belong to the same large category of mammals, the rodents, it's true. But so do hamsters, beavers, voles and dormice. The fact that grey squirrels (and red, too, though one rarely hears these being abused) have a taste for birds' eggs and the bark of young trees does not turn them into a different species.

The true rat of urban areas, the brown rat, is less easy to feel any affection for. Centuries of association with dirt and disease have made it virtually impossible to look at this creature objectively. Even in bald physical terms, though, he's hardly one of nature's beauties. Working from nose to tail you have a long and pointed face, large pink ears, coarse fur and a hairless rope of a tail. Brown rats weren't, as is often assumed, the species which played such a major role in spreading the Black Death in this country (this was the rarer black rat, which arrived here as a stowaway on ships returning from the Crusades). In fact they weren't known in Britain before the 1730s, when a population explosion in their native breeding grounds in Russia caused them to migrate and swarm over Western Europe. The first individuals almost certainly came over in ships that had been trading with Russia.

Brown rats are urban naturals. They hole up in canal banks,

rubbish dumps, industrial buildings, sewers, and particularly any store or warehouse where food is kept. They will eat anything, including each other if alternative foods are in short supply. One of the biggest London strongholds has always been Covent Garden Market, especially at Christmas. But as I write this the Market is scheduled for demolition, and there is some nervousness about where the rats may move to. They commute about the sewage network, and under pressure, could surface anywhere. Six hundred and fifty thousand rats were killed in London's sewers in just one winter during the War.

As well as being daring and effective raiders of food supplies, brown rats can be carriers of infectious diseases. Their fleas can carry the bubonic plague and were almost certainly the cause of the few hushed-up cases of plague that have occurred in the Port of London even in this century. They also carry a number of parasitic worms that can be passed to humans.

But for all this it's difficult not to have a sneaking admiration for the cheek and ingenuity of the brown rat. There's a story that when some years ago a row of rat-infested slum houses were demolished in London, the rats decamped to a nearby restaurant, and in an unnerving display of gluttony ran about on the tables snatching food from the plates. There is a more fascinating – if less voluntary – survival tactic in evidence in the London docks. There, in the cold stores which are kept at about minus 8°c, brown rats are able to flourish by growing an extra layer of fat and thicker fur – exactly the adaptation one finds in species dwelling permanently in the Arctic. (There are house mice in the cold stores too, which like thrifty gourmets, dine off bags of frozen kidneys and then nest in the resulting holes!)

Brown rats are also competent swimmers, which leads to some unfortunate cases of mistaken identity. Along one of the more industrialised stretches of the canal I worked this summer, I often used to come across factory workers spending their lunch-breaks using rats as target practice. The men would sit along the edge of the canal, sandwich in one hand and air-rifle in the other. Almost any living thing that passed along the cut would get potted at, swans included. But the full bombardments were reserved for any brown creature that was foolish enough to swim out from the holes that riddled the bank. Occasionally these were indeed brown rats, but since these largely go about their business by night and hide up during the day, they were more often innocent water voles, popularly known as water rats. Unhappily this name is as misleading and biologically inaccurate as 'tree rat' is for the grey squirrel. Voles are *not* rats and they follow a strict vegetarian diet. I remember vividly one I watched by the watercress beds, straining on tiptoe to reach some great willowherb leaves growing on top of a bank. At first he tried to nibble them in that position, but lost his footing, scrabbled the leaves down with his fore-paws, fell after them, and then began chewing them hamster-style, standing upright with the leaves grasped in his paws.

I suppose it may be expecting too great a sophistication of a non-biologist to distinguish the water vole from the brown rat by his short furry tail and blunt face. But there is no more telling lesson of the dangers of the loose naming of animals than the sight of one of these inoffensive creatures diving panic-stricken to escape the airgun pellets.

Rats, like pigeons, are of course acceptable if they are white – and confined in a cage. For all the town-dweller's apparent longing for the wild, on his home patch he seems to prefer it well and truly tamed. It's sobering to remember that less than a hundred years have passed since bird-catching was a flourishing trade in London. Goldfinches, linnets, and even nightingales were caught in large numbers for sale as caged songsters. This practice is now illegal thankfully, and it would be most unusual today to see a British song-bird in a pet-shop window. But our native mammals don't have anything like the legal protection afforded to birds, and, ironically, there's still a trade in orphan fox cubs from street-market pet stalls (those responsible for killing their parents having turned soft when it came to the young).

An animal pest is, like a weed, just a pet in the wrong place. Sometimes this is literally true. One August, for a local paper, I was looking into the colonisation of towns by foxes. There was not much gore and violence to be milked out of the story; but there was out of an extraordinary rash of outrages by the foxes' escaped domestic cousins, which erupted that same month and put the pest problem very firmly in perspective.

Foxes have always flourished on the edges of towns. They may get an irate hen-keeper's airgun raised at them occasionally, but they are considerably safer here than in the farming countryside. Their diet here, as elsewhere, is chiefly mice and rabbits. They will also take young birds in the breeding season and if pushed for food, beetles, frogs and even shellfish and fruit. (One in West Middlesex was found to have collected eight golf balls!) When they have the chance they will also plunder poultry runs, and often kill more birds than they need. But no fox which relied on this as its principal source of food would live for very long.

The foxes' increasingly regular forays into the towns themselves no doubt puts paid to a few more chickens and pet rabbits, though they seem chiefly interested in rooting about in dustbins. Yet that summer the authorities seemed bent on inventing a fox 'menace'. The Ministry of Agriculture revealed that their marksmen had been shooting an average of 200 animals a year in the Metropolitan fringes of Kent and Surrey. Foxes had been glimpsed sneaking up railway cuttings in the South London suburbs and ranging about the commons at dusk. They had even been reported in cemeteries in Wandsworth and Putney – no doubt adding to the widespread belief in their canny recognition of a safe wicket when they find one. (As did reports that they were plundering the emergency rubbish-tips set up during the dustmen's strike.) One Min. of Ag. spokesman predicted that 'if foxes are seen more frequently in town High Streets, I'm sure that local ratepayers will want some action.' Now there's no denying that the fox is a killer. But he's also arguably our handsomest mammal, blasé and disdainfully elegant, and whatever the Ministry may think, not everyone would find them unwelcome in their High Streets.

So what of the dog? The most alarming case I came across that month concerned a flock of 36 sheep wiped out in a single night by a gang of pets on the rampage. Sixteen sheep had been killed outright. Another twenty had to be destroyed because of injuries that would have done credit to the most vicious rogue fox. Some had had their ears and legs torn off. Others had been stampeded bodily straight through a barbed wire fence.

I'd also heard, from a town not a dozen miles away from the site of this episode, about a pack of strays attacking children. (You could add to this the perennial problem of pavement fouling, which except in the city centres puts the most regular pigeons to shame.)

They were grisly stories, I suppose, no worse and no better than could be told about any fox. This is the way animals live. We can't expect them to abide by our standards of good manners and morality. We make allowances for dogs because their nuisance value is outweighed by the pleasure they give to their owners. But creatures like foxes don't come off too well in this sort of calculation. They have no owners to plead on their behalf. When they are seen and enjoyed it is almost always a private experience. Yet on the few occasions when they do damage it is rapidly made a public affair. There ought surely to be a place in a city for a few colourful villains. There is no need even to see them. Just to know that they are there is enough, to lie in bed on a winter's night imagining those sharp muzzles sliding up the edges of the commuter tracks.

No creatures become labelled as pests until their numbers are sufficiently high for the nuisance they cause to be noticed. Normally, these numbers are kept down by natural predators. Take mice, for instance, in a moderately stable habitat like old woodland. Their numbers won't increase unless their food supplies increase *and* their natural enemies decrease. Any temporary growth in the mouse population will be taken care of by owls, weasels and so on, which will start to diet almost exclusively off the mice once they become numerous and easy to find.

The problem in urban areas is that there are very few natural predators, (though it wouldn't be unreasonable to regard man as one in man-made surroundings) but huge quantities of food for the creatures they normally prey off. So the prey populations increase until they are deliberately checked by man.

It's not easy to see why predators in urban areas don't build up populations to cope with those of their potential prey. London, for instance, would seem at first sight to be a natural home for peregrine falcons. The tall buildings apparently remind migrant birds sufficiently of their natural cliffside habitats for them to stop off on their autumn wanderings. And from St Paul's Cathedral, the Tower and the Barbican skyscrapers they've been watched causing havoc among the bemused local pigeons. You would think that with 20,000 pairs of their favourite game birds on tap, they would never leave the city. Yet they have never stayed to breed. Are peregrines too conservative in their choice of breeding sites to take up residence so far out of their usual range? Or is it the lack of some small but crucial factor like bathing sites that makes them ignore the well-stocked and cliff-like ledges of city buildings?

But we do have the kestrel, Gerard Manley Hopkins' 'windhover', whose flickering chestnut wings and tail fanned out against the wind are becoming a regular feature of the urban skyline. I was dogged by kestrels wherever I went that summer. So rarely did a day pass without my seeing one that they began to seem like mascots. I couldn't have asked for a more fitting one. There is no more magnificent or truly wild creature to be found in the built-up areas, nor one which has adapted so magnanimously to the most seedy and unwelcoming surroundings. There had been a kestrel that first day in spring, not quartering the rich commons, but poised over an allotment. Another had dashed down the centre of the Brompton Road in Chelsea. I had seen them hovering over a slum school playground in the docks, coasting round the top of Selfridges, hunting along a West London shunting yard, and ceaselessly quartering the waste ground by the side of the canal.

Anyone who has watched birds will know how it's possible to develop a special relationship with certain species. You begin to know, almost instinctively, when they are about, the weather in which they'll be moving, the particular corner of an apparently regular wood where they will be singing. This happened to me with my urban kestrels. I don't think of myself as a very technically accomplished birder. On most occasions when I go sea-watching, say, my binoculars are still wildly sweeping the horizon whilst my companions are sorting out whether the bird they have beaded is a guillemot or a razorbill. They have wisely learned to make allowances for my assumption that any vaguely-glimpsed bird is rare until proved common, and for all the half-hidden magpies mistaken for great grey shrikes, and distant crows for harriers.

Yet so much were my spirits raised every time I glimpsed that sharp profile against a grimy sky that I think I was imprinted as surely as any impressionable nestling kestrel. Often I would be deep in a book in a bus or train and suddenly find myself looking up. For a split second I wouldn't know why I'd raised my head. Then I'd see the cause, hunched on a telegraph pole or planing away behind me into a tree. It was a curious trick of peripheral vision, born no doubt of affection, that I've experienced with no other type of bird.

The most remarkable urban kestrel I ever saw was hovering about twenty feet above a traffic jam in the middle of a busy Outer London High Street. He seemed not to belong there, hanging over the lava flow of traffic, sliding a few feet to the side, flicking his wings and tail a few times for balance, then holding again. It is a prodigious feat of aerobatics, this moment when a kestrel hangs motionless in the air. He is in a perfectly controlled stall, a glide forward matched exactly against the speed of the wind. It is only when you see a hunting kestrel from the side, and see the habitually bowed head of the dog-end searcher that any of the mystery and dignity vanishes and he becomes a bird after a meal like any other.

But I was perplexed by what this High Street bird might be after. There seemed nowhere around that a mouse or vole might be hiding. It was only later that I learned a kestrel's eyes are so keen that at 50 feet above ground, say, it's capable of spotting – and eventually grabbing – prey over a hundred feet from the point above which it's poised. On this doubling-up principle, this bird ought to have been able to see nearly twenty yards away from the carriageway, which would have taken it well into the backyard and garden of a roadside pub.

Kestrels are unique amongst our birds of prey in their tolerance of human company and the change that inevitably goes with it. However much towns are razed to the ground, replanned, built up again, kestrels seem capable of finding a niche inside them. This may be a recent adaptation. Although at the beginning of the century they were the commonest bird-of-prey visitors to central London, none nested there. W. H. Hudson feared for their survival in the area.

Then, in the 1930s, birds began nesting regularly in inner London, on ledges and in the lofts of tall buildings. It wasn't a drastic change in behaviour, for even in open countryside kestrels are squatters. They don't build nests of their own but take over the abandoned quarters of other birds, squirrel dreys, holes in barn walls and so on.

Still, the list of some of their London residences is a splendidly democratic one: the Savoy Hotel, gasometers in the East End, Nelson's Column, the House of Lords, various power station chimneys and a ventilator shaft in Broadcasting House.

The most remarkable pair, though, were surely the ones that chose the window box of a sixteenth floor flat in a twenty-storey tower block in Peckham. They raised two young, but also the hackles of the flat owner, who boarded up the ledge next year because the birds were 'too messy'. Happily the kestrels decamped to the nearest suitable block down the road – and hopefully to a house-owner who was more grateful for such electrifying lodgers.

It may be in the availability of food that the answer to the kestrel's spread lies. Kestrels in the heavily built-up areas live largely off sparrows, which they take on the ground. As you move away from the city centres and the mammal population rises, the more their diet consists of mice and voles, until the proportion reaches something like 95 per cent in the farming countryside. The kestrel was one of the earliest birds of prey to be ruefully acknowledged as useful by gamekeepers. (Only out-of-the-ordinary individuals will ever take young pheasants and partridges.) The beginnings of the kestrel's increase in urban areas seemed to coincide with this greater tolerance. It's possible that conditions of real overcrowding began to develop in the countryside and that the more adaptable birds evacuated to the towns. And more recently, ironically, cities have been one of the few kinds of environment comparatively free of the agricultural pesticides that, concentrated down through the food chain, are so deadly to hawks.

Another act of enlightened tolerance had safeguarded some other urban predators five hundred years before. It was not until the early part of the fourteenth century that the streets of London were either paved or regularly cleaned. Dead dogs, kitchen refuse and excrement lay about quite openly. It's not surprising that London was home to countless scavenging birds, particularly the raven and that magnificent fork-tailed hawk, the kite. There were probably 100,000 kites in London in the Middle Ages, and they were so fearless that children used to feed them scraps of bread from the hand. By the middle of the fifteenth century the contribution that kites and ravens made towards keeping the streets clean had been officially recognised, and it was made a capital offence to kill them in London. The Act which protected them was the first piece of British nature conservation legislation which was not simply concerned to protect hunting rights.

But as the offal vanished, so did the kites. By the eighteenth century they had lost their privileged status, and in some areas there was even a bounty on their heads. The last pair probably nested in Hyde Park before the end of the century.

I find it disturbing to think of what might happen to kites if they should ever return to the city. With no useful function to perform would they get any better deal than the foxes? I suspect that Trafalgar Square's bird-fanciers might find their four-foot-span wings and meat-tearing beaks rather more daunting than did medieval children. And what would they make of peregrines, that would be more likely to take the pigeons out of their hands than the bread.

Our attitudes towards urban wildlife, our readiness to tolerate pests, is conditioned more than anything else by whether the creature in question will eat, both literally and metaphorically, out of our hands. No doubt foxes would be regarded as acceptable if they came sweetly, by day, to lap milk from doorstep saucers. Being lone wolves, midnight ramblers, prowlers and looters, they are branded as outlaws. It is homo sapiens' old chauvinism again: we are the stewards; animals should live by our rules, not those of the jungle. It's not one of our most consistent attitudes.

*

Parks

I wish to express my disappointment at the organisation,
layout, inmates and general concept of the so-called Wild
Animal Kingdom at Woburn.

It took my friends and I approximately three and a
half hours to drive through the four-mile route. We were
accompanied by several other cars sometimes driving four
abreast, which would make it virtually impossible for the
occupants of the middle rows of cars to see the 'savage'
animals snoring away in some corner anything from ten to
50 yards away (one wag rumoured that they were stuffed). I
have seen more life in the British Museum.

from a letter in the *Herts Evening Echo*

I spent some weeks that summer wandering around town parks.
They were a motley collection and at times I couldn't fathom just
what those responsible for them were trying to achieve. I suppose
there are such things as wholly urban parks (as distinct from parks
in urban areas), with nothing more than kiosks, parasols, bandstands
on concrete piazzas, roundabouts for the children and seats for
their mums. But most appear to be making at least some gesture at
introducing a little natural life. Parks, unlike so many of the other
green patches we have looked at so far, are *deliberate* attempts to
create artificial packages of country inside the towns. But how many
really have any of the qualities that we associate with the countryside
– the qualities that town-dwellers seem to want, to judge from their
weekend flights into the countryside proper?

In old churchyards and newly planted recreation grounds, I would
sit poker-backed on the slatted seats, wondering whether the 'Keep
Off' signs really made me feel deprived of the baked and shaven turf,
and work through a mental tariff of these qualities. I freely admit
that I was looking round me chiefly as a naturalist. That was why

I was there. But I believe that the needs of the nature freak, of the creatures he is after, and of those who have simply come to stroll or loll about after a day in the office – nearly ninety per cent of all park users – are not as different as they are often made out to be.

Peace and quiet, for one, and at least some respite from the noise and stench of exhaust fumes. If you don't suffer from agoraphobia and can venture into the very centre of a big park you may just capture a little of this. But how many smaller parks screen their perimeters with noise-absorbing bushes instead of those forbidding iron railings? Many of them look more like exercise yards than play areas. What better and more delightfully surprising place could there be to find a traditional English hedgerow than round the edge of public open space? Heaven knows, they are vanishing fast enough just about everywhere else.

There would be a bonus too in the songs of the birds that would move in to breed. No matter that most of the singers would be blackbirds and thrushes. They are amongst our best songsters anyway, and a lunch-hour stroller is not after making lists of rarities. But you'll not hear much song from a park where the only birds which can find a place to nest are sparrows with a taste for park-keepers' toolsheds.

If a backcloth of bird-song is one breath of country grace that would please most park users, so might be the chance to pick a few flowers. No one wants to encourage the plundering of decreasing species like primroses, which are now rare in urban areas precisely because they have been over-picked. But there's no harm – and probably a great deal of good – in physical contact with the commoner plants. Looking at a flower only tells you half its story. You need, too, to be able to bury your nose in its pollen and feel the texture of its petals – and, perhaps, be a harvester for a while.

But there is little chance of this in most municipal parks. The meticulous flowerbeds, as spectacularly fragile and short-lived in their successions as a public firework display, are forbidden. The wild flowers and fruits are all but extinct. Brambles and raspberries disappear under the flail-mowers, and the buttercups, dandelions and daisies, which bloom the more frenziedly when they are hand-picked, vanish as the grass is shorn to putting-green smoothness and sterilised by selective weedkillers:

> I have seen three city girls sent crazy-drunk in springtime by the unknown, unexpected sight and smell of unfenced Council-laid-out beds of tossing daffodils, so that they rushed at them and picked them and threw them all in the air, like an ecstatic puppy in one's arms will gobble up a bunch of violets, quite out of their senses – or maybe at last in them.
>
> I have seen children in a park warned off from picking blossom, encouraged by a sympathetic adult to pick the dandelions that grew among the grass, thinking that was safe for them. But I saw the dandelions whipped away from them by an outraged keeper who scourged them with withering words, and then before the children's agonised eyes, rammed the flowers into a rubbish bin, smashing them down righteously to make sure they could not be rescued or revived.
>
> The children on Council estates cannot keep animals, and cannot grow flowers. I am sure children need to be in touch with the earth, need to have their fingers in soil, and their eyes looking into an animal's, or a bird's eyes. These children are dissociated from the universe, and the rhythm of the universe.
>
> *Look at Kids* by Leila Berg, 1972

And what of The View, that even if all the nice (and to some no doubt cissy) extras of birds and blossoms are forgotten, no one who enters a park would want to be without? Well, in too many there is none at all. The ground is unrelentingly flat. There is no point where you can suddenly rise up and see a horizon, none of those secret and unexpected glades that are commonplace in so many patches of unplanned waste ground. The trees, if the pruned and emaciated shrubs that are planted in these places can be called trees, march on in lines as regular as if they were in a nursery. Stand at any point in the park and your view is much the same.

I once had an insight into one of the things that is wrong with modern park planning whilst I was travelling on a train through outer London. The carriage window had framed a field as square and flat and bare as a football pitch, save for a dead straight row of skinny poplars. Next to the field was a crop of tower blocks as geometrically drilled as the trees. It was a pitiful scene, like one of those architect's models with baize grass and cotton wool shrubs. You could see that this plot, like so many other urban open spaces, had been planned on just those spartan principles it was presumably meant to provide some relief from: hard edges, smooth surfaces, squareness, and regimentation, even down to the rigid time-tabling that shepherds the public in and out as relentlessly as if they were travelling on a bus route.

The natural world, mercifully, does not work by rules as rigid and soulless as these – and which even we, as biological creatures ourselves at heart, go out into the countryside to escape. It is responsive, as we are, to the weather and the seasons. Birds sing in the warm weather and work hard for food in the cold. Flowers open their petals more seductively for the insects in the sun, and sometimes close up altogether when the sky is overcast. Neither hunting foxes nor migrating birds have any respect for night-time curfews. Nor does anything in nature grow in straight lines. A bank of wild flowers will gush forward in one place, cower in a second and rocket inexplicably towards the heavens in a third. A man is no different. Ask him to walk in as straight a line as he can muster between two landmarks in a grassy meadow, and the track he leaves will be as softly curved as a bend in a stream.

There is a need for these life-reflecting qualities in a park just as much as for the swings and rhododendron patches that delight the young and old. But they can be emasculated by the pruning knife and the mowing machine, and by those conscientious park-keepers who sweep up the fallen leaves before you have a chance to scuff them about and realise that it is autumn again. A park managed like this is little more than an estate where the building materials just happen to be living, forcibly kept in a state of permanent hibernation.

Not all parks are like this. Regent's Park in London, for instance, is big and varied enough to be both a well-ordered playground and an urban wilderness. Much of it is as I have already described. Yet the cow parsley puts up as good a show as the planted daffs in some of the enclosures. There are fine old hardwood trees for tawny owls and squirrels and an abundance of fruiting shrubs, which provide nesting sites and food galore for the 20 or so species of song birds that breed in the park every year. Britain's most newsworthy bird, the osprey, has been seen circling over the ponds in August, and that dapper warbler, the blackcap breeds in some of the more overgrown patches. Most surprising of all was the visit in September 1965, by a water pipit, a lark-like bird probably on migration to France from its Baltic breeding grounds, which was seen picking at a discarded butter wrapping.

The wildest place in Regent's Park is the big pond with its inaccessible wooded island. Giant hogweed has secreted itself in here as well, coralled off out of hand's reach by water and railings, though no less malevolently showy because of that. But it is quite upstaged by the herons. In winter herons are frequent visitors to urban ponds, which stay unfrozen in the higher temperatures of cities for some while longer than open water in the countryside. The pool in Regent's Park has always been especially popular with these refugee herons. One year a solitary bird even stayed over for the spring, and suffering apparently from sympathetic broodiness, was seen building a makeshift nest on the roof of the captive herons' cage in the nearby Zoo.

But this summer a group of the birds had unexpectedly chosen this tiny copsed island to set up central London's first heronry. Those who had access to the island found that there were a dozen nests. Most were high up in the trees, and herons' nests being the ungainly and twiggy hammocks they are, could be seen quite easily from the edge of the lake. I could pick out nine as I sat on a bench one glorious afternoon early in July, and in a few I could see the lanky young birds trying their wings. To feed them the parent birds apparently cleaned out most of the goldfish ponds in London!

It was marvellous to see these great grey birds beating heavily away for their next feed, creatures of gaunt fens loping over the bright and busy shrubs of a city playground. But curiously it was not so much these heavy flights that brought a hint of marshland wildness to this scene, as the birds' motionless vigils on the trees overhanging the lake. I watched one standing sentinel on the end of a dead thorn branch for over an hour, as sharp and posed against the citrus fronds of the weeping willows as a bird in a Japanese print. Against the bathtub ducks scuttering after their bread it was this inscrutable patience that spoke most tellingly of the rigours of life in the wild.

But it is Hampstead Heath, that expanse of wild country rising as refreshingly and miraculously as a mirage out of mile upon mile of besieging concrete, that is for me the finest example of what an urban park can be. Hampstead's hilliness has always been its greatest asset. To reach its highest point you must climb over 500 feet in two miles. In the days when the air was cleaner they said you could see the steeple of Hanslope church from the top, over fifty miles away in Buckinghamshire. There was even a delightfully Heath Robinson plan to pump air in pipes down from the balmy heights to the choking citizens in the City below.

Hampstead Heath also lies on poor, sandy soil, which in town and country alike gives a piece of ground a fair chance of remaining undeveloped. Being of little agricultural use in pre-industrial times, this sort of ground was usually given over as common land, a status which the commoners would stoutly defend (with clubs and fists on more than one occasion) whilst more secure farmers were selling off their land to the property sharks. Luckily the era of industrial sprawl and ruthless property development sparked off a concern for the recreational value of open space, and the guerrilla commoners often found they had enlightened planning authorities on their side. The ironic result of this was that many patches of poor land remained open whilst the rich surrounding farmland was built on.

This is no place to go into the complex and interminable legal wrangles which led up to the saving of Hampstead Heath for the public. But there are some points in the story which do suggest the sort of qualities people want from their parks, if they are given the chance to determine them.

Up to the beginning of the nineteenth century Hampstead Heath was as busy and varied a place as you could imagine. Contemporary prints suggest that it looked much like the dry and furzy heaths that still exist in sandy areas of Surrey and East Anglia. What is different is the flurry of human activity that's apparent. The two principal common uses of the heath were laundering and donkey grazing. The laundresses, in true rustic style, used to spread their washing out on to the gorse bushes to dry. There was also a certain amount of sand-digging for the building trade, and military training (another perennial fate of sandy ground).

But if the soil was too poor for cultivated crops it was certainly not for the wild flora. The Heath had one of the best and most varied collections of wild flowers in the neighbourhood of the city, and they were highly valued. The Society of Apothecaries used to take parties of their apprentices for rambles over the Heath (no overcoats or umbrellas allowed) to give them a handy round-up of the medicinal plants they would be dealing with. Earlier the Heath had been one of the favourite hunting grounds of the founding fathers of herbalism. Gerard, Parkinson, Ray and Hudson all botanised there. But it was Thomas Johnson, the man who discreetly reworked Gerard's maverick *Herball* until it was a work of scientific respectability as well as a delightful and fanciful impression of our flora, who made the most famous expeditions.

In short it was a place for all manner of tastes and activities, laborious and leisurely alike. But at the beginning of the nineteenth century, Sir Thomas Maryon Wilson, the Lord of the Manor of Hampstead, cast his eye on the potential for property development in such a salubrious area (it was also fashionable as a Spa) and began a campaign to start building on the Heath. Years of Bills and counter-petitions in the Commons and Lords followed, the upshot of which was that Sir Thomas's plans were thwarted. That this was a result more of the pressure from rich middle-classes who lived on the edge of the Heath than the anger of the vast bulk of ordinary commoners just goes to show that the politics of conservation haven't changed very much.

In a fit of pique, Sir Thomas began a work-to-rule. He exercised his rights to charge those who hung out washing or grazed their geese on the Heath. He planted out acres of open ground with willows and firs, and carted sand away in ever increasing quantities. He opened up more brickfields and new roads in the East.

The ratepayers of Hampstead were incensed and the legal wrangles began again. In 1857 a writer who in all probability was Charles Dickens, weighed in against Sir Thomas in the magazine *Household Words*, and talks of:

a number of infantile trees, cased in with wooden hurdles ...
Who planted them? Had they any business to do so? They
are an eyesore. Where will they end? Did not some one say
that somebody – we forget, and do not care who – tried to
enclose Hampstead Heath? If he does so, may his heirs find
a quick road to their inheritance! ... It must have been some
half-fledged baronet, the second of the family, who having
half title to his own property, fancied that no tide at all
might suffice for appropriating that of the public. Whoever
he was, may his dreams be redolent of Smithfield, may
nightmare tread with donkey hoofs on his chest, and may
visions of angry laundresses scald his brain with weak tea!

Shades of John Clare's poem against the agricultural enclosures,
when he mourned for the days when:

> Unbounded freedom ruled the wandering scene
> Nor fence of ownership crept in between
> To hide the prospect of the following eye
> Its only bondage was the circling sky
> One mighty flat undwarfed by bush and tree

It was a stroke of vision to see that this urban landscape, too,
heathy by nature, riding like a downland scarp above the tight-
packed buildings, also needed its space and its views.

Eventually – and perhaps largely because of the death of Sir
Thomas – the Metropolitan Board of Works were able to purchase
the Manorial rights of the Heath. In 1871 the historic Hampstead
Heath Act was passed. In the face of the prettification that was
going on in parks all over Victorian England, this stated firmly
and clearly in its preamble that it would be 'of great advantage to
the inhabitants of the Metropolis if the Heath were always kept
unenclosed and unbuilt on, *its natural aspect and state being as far
as may be preserved*' (my italics).

Unfortunately those responsible for the Heath did not seem to
understand the spirit of those words, and in 1896 the London County

Council began, like any modern Parks Dept. gardener hoeing his begonia beds, to 'tidy up' the Heath. No doubt it was a well-meant action, but nothing short of wholesale devastation or redevelopment could have been more contrary to the intentions of the Act, or to the character of that obstinately wild place. They cut and burned the gorse, filled in hollows and bogs, and as if nothing had been learned from the last fifty years, began planting trees in their hundreds in the Upper East Heath. The outcry these so-called improvements set off was nationwide, and was more popularly based than any of the previous movements to conserve the Heath. A Hampstead Heath Protection Society was quickly formed, and was able to hold back the worst of the gardening. But it was twenty years before they were able to persuade the London County Council to thin the trees and reopen some of the lost glades and views.

I think the Heath then must have been much as I found it when I visited it late that July. It was the first time I had explored it thoroughly, and I was astonished at how quickly this feeling of wildness enveloped one. It was a hot day, and the soldier beetles were working the hogweed flowers. Less than twenty yards off the road I was wading through knee-high meadow and rye grass. Then on to those glorious open slopes, that fill your lungs and make you want to plunge off at a gallop through the grass. I restrained myself and sat on the edge of one of the hollows to watch the birds. It was not too comfy a seat, for the plants of these very dry and sandy places are a thin and scrawny lot. There were tiny mats of heath bedstraw and the halberd-leaved sheep's sorrel. But it was a good prospect in front of me. A damp valley just at the foot of the slope, picked out by a line of oaks and willows, and patches of scrub to my left and right.

I was surprised at just how much bird song there was considering it was late in the season. In the distance I could hear the knife-whetting call of a chiffchaff, a blackcap, and once, briefly, the laugh of a green woodpecker. Swifts were haring after flies only inches from the ground, sometimes passing so near me that I could hear the rush of their wings. It was good to see them so close to the centre of the city, along with the house martins that were flitting more leisurely above the tree-tops. That such voraciously insectivorous birds should have been hunting there in force was probably due in no small measure to the cleaning-up of London's air. In the ten years following the Clean Air Act of 1956, the smoke content of London's air was reduced by nearly two thirds.

The next bird was no surprise to me, though he might have been to anyone else. He had followed me there, like everywhere else. The black-tipped chestnut wings, the slips to the side as he jigged through the slalom of trees, were unmistakeable. I don't think he was hunting seriously, as he flickered purposefully off towards a nearby church. I saw two kestrels frequently that day, this male bird and a female, heading off each time in the same direction, and I guess they may have been sharing a church nesting site with the swifts.

For once I felt I ought to follow the kestrel rather than let him haunt me, and I dropped down into the valley. The dampness is due to a springline which runs along the boundary between the sandy hills and the deeper layers of impervious London Clay. It was a delight following the rushy contours of this watercourse, for they were embroidered with as pretty a collection of marsh plants as you could wish to find. There were flowers that I had seen already along the canals: gipsywort, yellow flags, now in full bloom with their splendid iris blossoms and tall leaf spears, great willow herb, the remains of spring-flowering marsh marigolds, and unless I was mistaken the beginnings of one of the rarest plants of the Heath, the marsh pennywort, a skulking creeper of dank boggy places, whose small coin-like leaves are attached to their stalks in the very centre, toadstool-style. But the most pleasing of all was a single spike of amphibious bistort, not unlike the flowerhead of a buddleia. And all these clustered in dells and hollows at the foot of a knot of willows – a fen only twenty yards from one of the Heath's through roads.

Following the spring in the other direction led me deeper and deeper into damp scrub. It seemed pointlessly timid to stay to the paths in such a place, so I began to scrabble through the dense bushes. In a while I came to the realisation that after four months' ferreting round labyrinthine gravel pits and overgrown wastelands hundreds of acres in extent, I had got myself lost in a public park.

Of course I was not really lost. If I had walked a straight quarter-of-a-mile in any direction I could not have failed to strike a road, or at least a well-used path. But the illusion was there. I could see and hear not a single human sound. I had no idea what lay in front of me, nor the direction I ought to take to get out of this swamp. It is chastening to have this experience once in a while. It reminds you of your place – which in the countryside, unlike the town, is usually as an ill-adapted, clumsy intruder. I was given a sharp and sudden lesson in how literally true this is when I suddenly went down to my knees in the mud. I really ought to have known better, I decided, eyeing the tell-tale rust-coloured films on the soil as I dragged my suèdes clear. It was no excuse to say that those few seconds of disorientation had made me quicken my pace. Yet I was a little proud of my caked jeans. I'd got my hands dirty – or at least my feet – some sort of evidence of a job done. Weeks of watching from comfortable Greenline seats and park benches had made me feel a little soft and guilty.

Feeling smug about my hard morning down t'park lasted just until I took my lunchtime pint, and the broiling July sun started to make me smell like a sewerworker. I retired to a dark corner of the pub in some embarrassment – which was just as well, since as anyone who has ever had their feet caked with bog mud will have predicted, itches started of such devastation that I had to rip my shoes and socks off and dry my feet with pages torn from my notebook. And burning a hole on my lap were those damned binoculars again. I began to feel like a thinly disguised bumpkin spy parachuted down in the wrong country.

But that spell of sobering – if not sober – drying-out was some way off yet. There were the woods to the north still to be explored, cool, spacious groves of oak, birch and chestnut. The paths into them were thickly grassed, good for wiping the mud off, and worn to just the openness they needed by the walkers who used them. There was not much ground vegetation left inside the woods themselves, and no sign of the bluebells and wood anemones that once grew here in profusion. But at least the ground was honest soil, not yet plastered over with asphalt or gravel paths. I found two new balsams here, the small yellow in a dark corner, and some young shoots of the Himalayan balsam (known as policeman's helmet from the shape of its bell-shaped flowers) at the edge of one of the wood bogs, which for the benefit of the footloose, are clearly marked in these open areas by red signs. And there were nuthatches, crisp blue and chestnut, trilling in the top branches.

I was allowed one more treat before departing to show off my ham-footedness, when I tracked down a grey squirrel by his querulous chatter. He was up in the top of an old hawthorn, only feet away from his drey – which could well have contained young at this time of year and accounted for the creature's peevish slanging. He was a wild and stringy fellow, not at all like his elegant cousins in Regent's Park, and he delivered his abuse leaning forward on the branch to curse me more effectively.

After lunch I passed out of the woods into country that reminded me of the heaths in East Anglia. There were stands of Scots pine and false acacia, and steep paths as scrabbly as sand dunes winding up through fists of gorse ablaze with coconut-scented flowers. It was good to break out on to the high open ground again and see the tangled architecture of the Heath falling away and merging with the buildings on the horizon. From this vantage point I could see just about every component of the place: the slopes and changes of texture in the grass, the thickets and strips of woodland, even the human inhabitants. One thing was plain from this high viewpoint; some of the young trees will have to be thinned out before long if the Heath is to keep its special character. It was painful to be made aware of this, for it had been a delight to find urban oaks regenerating naturally when they are being hacked down so relentlessly in rural areas. But Charles Dickens was right to see the Heath as a place of space and sky. (Just as W. H. Hudson was right to fume *against* the barbaric felling of seven hundred mature elms in Kensington Gardens at the end of the last century. They were the tallest trees in London, home of a vast rookery, a true urban wood on a flat site where no other style of landscape could have easily injected a feeling of wildness. How old the tradition for municipal fussiness is! The reason given by the Park authorities for this act of vandalism was that grass would not grow – and presumably therefore could not be mown – under the shade of the elms, and people could not walk about in those parts of the park without soiling their shoes.)

Hampstead Heath has something for everyone. Scrub and woodland for birdwatchers, bogs for botanists, ponds for swimmers and anglers (and for sparrows, who scrump the latter's ground-bait), rough paths for walkers and rough grass for lovers. And round the edges of the open heath, not intruding on its sense of wildness, are the stately homes, ornamental gardens and bowling greens. There have been conflicts between all these elements. As one advances another must retreat, and the management has not always mediated between them very sensibly. But overall I think that the Heath has succeeded as one of our greatest urban parks precisely because it has not been designed on a drawing board but within reason has been allowed to develop naturally. And by that I don't mean that it is the product of a crude policy of laissez-faire, but that the patterns of development which unfold in environments like the Heath when they are in semi-wild countryside, have been allowed to proceed unchecked, and in some cases been deliberately copied. So hollows become ponds, and unmown lawns meadows. The result is that Hampstead has maybe the closest approximation to the feel of the countryside that you could find inside a city.

There are no more than a handful of similar open spaces in our cities. Cattle graze in Crossacres Park, in Manchester. A park in Chelmsford produces crops of willows for a local cricket bat factory. In Glasgow, one of the most harshly urban cities in Britain, they now have a network of walkways threading their green and subversive way between the tenement blocks and dockyards. Any abandoned passageway can be turned into a link in this rural underground – a canal, a derelict railway line, a drove-way of felled slums snatched up by the Parks Department before the property developers could get their hands on the land. The walkways are kept as wild as possible. There are no neatly straightened paths and only sufficient lopping and pruning to keep the way open. Moss and weeds are tolerated and there has been a massive transplantation of mature trees to give the ways a kind of built-in history.

How good it would be to see similar schemes in operation in all our cities. Why not orchards and working farms in the bigger parks? Even small artificial hills could be made quite easily with modern earth-shifting equipment. Heaven knows, there is enough soil gouged out of the urban areas for the sake of shunting people round a little quicker, that there would be a touch of justice in putting it back in the places where they go to slow down.

But it is trees above all else that are needed to break up the hard-edged texture of urban living. Nothing can compete with these larger-than-life organisms for signalling the changes in the natural world. They are barometers – not just to the weather but to the changes of the seasons. Leaves change colour, fall and reappear. In winter branches provide a scaffolding for the traceries of hoar-frost. The motion of trees is part of our very experience of wind, making something substantial out of what is so often just felt as a chilling draught or a faceful of dust. There are men who have worked in forests who say they can tell the species of a tree from the sounds it makes in the wind.

They have more humdrum uses too. They can shade us on hot days and shelter us from the rain. And then there are the colours, the pastel grey-greens and waxy emeralds, the mottled old-golds and dying browns. There are no shades as restful and as subtle as these in the town planners' paint catalogues.

For wildlife trees are crucial. They are one of the major food sources for the insects on which birds and higher animals depend. And when, inside towns, rows of them stitch the streets together – as hedges do the patchwork fields of the farming landscape – they form a food chain of a different sort for birds and insects, a bountiful natural road system that can provide a lifeline between town and country.

Cities should be bursting with trees. They should surround every drab playing field and rubbish dump. They should line the roads and range along the middles of dual carriageways (where they would be useful as well as attractive). Back in Glasgow they have planted roundabouts with traditional Scottish plants like heather, bilberry and silver birch. There is no obvious reason why we too shouldn't plant native trees like the oak and the ash in areas where their size would not be a danger to traffic or to the foundations of buildings. Instead, our indigenous trees are the most harassed of all. On the flimsiest of excuses – a hint of fungus, the blotting out of a few square feet of sunlight – down they come, three hundred years of growth wiped out as casually as if it were already a disposable packing material. All too often urban trees are felled by householders in flagrant contradiction of their neighbours' wishes and sometimes of Tree Preservation Orders. (Two Cedars of Lebanon near my house went this way. The felling was irrevocably under way early in the morning before anyone was about.) Even local councils seem to work on a policy of fell first and face the protests later – then placate them with a few tame and manageable shrubs.

Over a hundred years ago Richard Jefferies was wise to this view that the proper role for trees in urban parks and gardens was as dinky ornaments:

> Though such suburban grounds mimic the isolation and
> retirement of ancient country-houses surrounded with parks,
> the distinctive feature of the ancient houses is omitted.
> There are no massed bodies, as it were, of our own trees to
> give substance to the view. Are young oaks ever seen in the
> grounds so often described as park-like? . . . The oaks that
> are there drop their acorns in vain, for if one takes root it is
> at once cut off; it would spoil the laurels.
>
> *Nature Near London*, 1879

But cities are cosmopolitan by nature, and there is a place for globe-trotting and exotic trees: catalpas and pagodas and that extraordinary freak, the ginkgo. Although the few specimens of this which grow round London were introduced from Japan, it was indigenous here some millions of years ago. It is a frothy, cedar-like tree with a bark that's been likened to an elephant's hide, and leaves like those of a giant maidenhair fern. Sometimes peg-like burrs develop on the trunk, extend down to the ground, take root and form new plants.

The most familiar alien tree in urban areas is the plane, the first varieties of which were brought to this country from Asia in the sixteenth century. Its popularity in urban and industrial areas is probably due to its extreme hardiness and tolerance of poor soils and polluted air. It's a clean tree, too, having shiny leaves which are quickly washed free of soot by rain, and sloughing off its grimy bark at intervals to leave fresh fawn layers underneath. (Though contrary to popular belief this isn't some hygienic measure helping it to survive in smoggy airs.) But given the authorities' customary attitude towards pests, it's a paradox that the plane has been so continuously popular. The pollen shed by its fuzzy fruits in the early spring is an increasing cause of hay-fever, and the huge leathery leaves which fall after a heavy autumn frost can bury pavements inches deep. And for my taste the plane hasn't quite the right style for a city tree, being too spacious and bony. Yet it's not without its place in the natural community. Its leaves are the chief food plant of vapourer moth caterpillars, formidably hairy creatures that hatch into the tiny brown moths that can often be seen dithering about town streets in spring.

The type of urban recreational land most likely to provide some all-round country comforts is the golf-course (which, incidentally, occupy 2 per cent of all Green Belt land). Consider what a golfer wants from his links. He will not be attracted by a course in which the holes are indistinguishable and the degree and class of skill needed for each are identical. He is after variety, risk, challenge, a chance to show his flexibility and range, and, let's hope, a backcloth of agreeable scenery against which to play his game. Most of this is summed up for the players in the notion of *hazards* – clumps of trees, gorse thickets and ponds. To wildlife, of course, these are anything but hazards. Although ground-nesting species can't tolerate the continual disturbance, linnets and yellowhammers thrive in the scrub between the fairways, and don't seem too put out by the odd stray balls from novice drivers that plummet into their territories.

The mown sections of the course carry a quite different range of habitats, down-like on the fairways, and heathy or meadowy in the rough, depending on the nature of the underlying soil. Golf-courses are often constructed on well-drained chalk or sands because these soils produce a finer turf than the heavier clays. They're good botanising ground as a result, for dry grasslands are amongst the very best habitats we have for wild flowers in our island.

It was on a hilly chalk course that I went flower-hunting late in

July. It was a small links on the edge of a sprawling New Town, and was coiled round the slopes of the only chalk outcrop within a ten mile radius. Those who built the course had made the classic planning reaction to shortage of groundspace, and had extended upwards. So what the holes lost in length they made up for in rise. So, embarrassed to be empty-handed for once, I toiled up the edges of the fairways between the braces of players. It is a marvel to me, as a non-golfer, the pains the groundsmen take to provide almost minutely different challenges for the players. The greens of course were of the finest and closest mown grasses, probably not more than two species at the most, and almost devoid of life above ground as a result. The fairways were better, and carried the sort of flowers you would expect to find on a lightly-mown lawn. (I have seen woodcocks prising out worms from the fairways in more rural areas.) But it was in what I suppose may be called the smooth-rough at the edge of the fairways that the flowers warmed up. This is where, in order to give the players something to battle with, the mowers raise their blades to about six inches above the ground. This keeps the fast-growing, coarse grasses in check and give the squat downland herbs a chance to prosper. To the passing foursomes I must have looked demented, poking about in this open grass. I had done a bit of lost-golf-ball hunting myself when I was a boy (we could get 6d each for them at the local sports shop), and I knew how they were summing up my bowed head and crooked meanderings. Only a blind man could lose a ball in grass like this, and a fool look for one.

What I did find had a lower market value than golf balls but was a considerably greater delight to my eye. There were milkworts, salad burnet, whose leaves smelt deliciously of cucumber as I walked over them, floppy yellow rock-rose flowers, bunches of wild thyme, alive with bees, and the blue bells of the wild campanula. But I must confess I didn't give these blooms the attention they deserved. My eye was set with all the lustful single-mindedness of a treasure-hunter after just one type of flower. Orchids. It's a mystery the spell that orchids weave over plant lovers. If the truth were told those which grow in this country are not that uniquely beautiful. The best orchid field you ever see will not match the sheer dense brilliance of a railway embankment deep in rosebay willowherb. No orchid has a scent to match the common honeysuckle or a colour that can outshine the deep mulberry of purple loosestrife. Look closely at a red dead-nettle and you won't find the blossoms less charming or intricate than those of a spotted orchid.

Yet the magic of orchids persist, for laymen and botanists alike. I doubt if there is a single wildflower lover who does not venture out to his nearest stretch of chalk down or beechwood in June or July to look especially for these plants. Is it all due to those awesome hothouse orchids from the tropics? A little relic of sentimentality perhaps, hanging on from a wedding bouquet or a special button hole, and passed on by association to all those bearing the family name? Is it the stories of those piratical orchid hunters who were sent out by the nurserymen in the nineteenth century to plunder the jungles of four continents? Or the uncanny resemblances which orchid flowers often bear to other creatures: bearded hillbillies, red spiders, flying ducks in Australia, laughing gnomes and eyelashes in South America, scorpions in S. E. Asia, and back in Britain, monkeys, bees, soldiers, butterflies and frogs? It may be though that some sense of the life-cycle of the orchid, surely one of the most extraordinary in the plant world, has helped colour our attitude towards these flowers.

In most flowers the development of the plant from seed to leaf follows a brisk and fairly straightforward path. The seeds are large enough to feed the seedling until it breaks through into the light, develops green leaves and is able to start manufacturing its own nourishment by photosynthesis.

It's not such a simple road for an infant orchid, which is literally a retarded developer. The seeds are so small and contain so little food reserves that for many species it is a matter of years (not weeks as with most flowers) before anything resembling a seedling with leaves appears above ground. Most plants would die of starvation if they took this long before they had the opportunity to start manufacturing their own foods. But by one of those ironic freaks of evolution, the laborious inchings of the underground orchid plant are fuelled by a fungus, which, in spite of the diminutive size of the orchid seeds, voraciously attacks them. This fungus is not unlike a mildew and penetrates deep into the tissues of the seed.

Now the common factor amongst all fungi, from the most monstrous puffball to a microscopic mould, is that they contain no chlorophyll. They therefore cannot manufacture their own sugars and other energy-producing foods. Their survival depends on obtaining nourishment from green plants (which are still producing it) or the dead remains of living creatures (which have it stored up). The fungi which invade the tiny roots of orchid seedlings obtain most of their food from the abundant remnants of dead plants in the soil. This is circulated around the fungus, including those parts which are living more frugally off the toiling orchid seedling. But this is the irony: so intimately meshed are the tissues of the fungus and the orchid that the latter is able to filch some of the fungus's food and supplement its own natural supplies. It seems, in fact, as if the first assault by the fungus acts like a blood transfusion on an ailing and undernourished child. The orchid seedling, picking up food and strength from the fungus, can grow sufficiently to fight back against the fungus and sometimes succeeds in containing it within a restricted territory inside itself. The fungus, still receiving supplies from behind the lines as it were, then mounts a counter-attack against its now more succulent prey.

And so this tug-of-war continues, sometimes with the orchid seedling in the ascendant, sometimes the fungus, depending on external conditions in the soil. Countless orchid seedlings are obliterated in the process. But a few gain the upper hand, and over a period of time (as much as fifteen years in some orchids) have grown sufficiently to push leaf shoots through the ground. Once it has reached this stage the orchid is in a much happier position. Instead of having to rely on the fungus for its food supplies it can manufacture its own by photosynthesis in its green leaves.

It isn't easy to sum up this relationship between orchid and fungus. It's not simply parasitism, for no host ever got the advantages from a parasite that the orchid seedling gets from that vampyric mould. Nor is it symbiosis, that relationship which natural history encyclopaedias describe as 'two organisms living together for their mutual advantage'. That's altogether too cosy a description of the bitter and protracted struggle that's going on beneath the ground. Though the seedling does gain its maturity by virtue of the assault, it's just as likely to be bumped off. And there's no advantage to the fungus at all in moving in on these seedlings; it could live just as well sticking to dead plant material. I think one is forced to be anthropomorphic to find a situation analogous to this curious relationship – perhaps in one of those bitter but intense marriages where the more intimate and fierce their fighting, the more the partners seem to prosper, preying off each other's renewing strength.

So in the unofficial countryside, orchids are the greatest prize of all. It is a miracle if their laborious and fragile growth cycle can find the peace and time it needs amidst the constant harassment of the ground that is the norm in the built-up zone. Golf-courses are one of the few areas where the primary users of the ground have as great a respect for the turf as any botanist.

So orchids were what I was on the lookout for on the links that July day. And one species in particular, the frog orchid. Frog orchids are not common even on mature downland in the open countryside, and this course had reputedly the only remaining colony in the county. My local Flora even gave helpful descriptions of how to find the site. They were almost like treasure-hunt notes, with a map reference, specifications of the slope of the hill, and the number of paces from the fence. I did as I was told, and though I'm no scout, I think I ended up where the orchids were supposed to be. I had found frog orchids before on the Berkshire Downs, and I knew them as small and surprisingly inconspicuous plants, scarcely standing out at all amongst the short grass they favour. So I quartered the slope carefully, eyes close to my feet, and going down on hands and knees in the more promising patches. But not an orchid could I find, though there were other downland flowers a-plenty.

I trudged on round the course, poking about in the few patches of grass that had not been close-mown. Most of these were the steepish slopes that lay at the back of the greens, the result of the scalloping out of these flat surfaces from the hills. I didn't notice whether in fact it was the ninth and final green where I struck lucky, but my patience was running out and it was certainly the last one I was going to play. But there, nestling under a foot-tall birch shrub, I spied a couple of skulking frogs. I crawled about the area, expecting a horrified 'fore' to ring in my ears at any second, and found a couple of dozen plants growing in an area not more than two yards square. Some, I swear, were no more than twelve inches from the crew-cut lawn of the greens.

Scarce flowers don't often live up to the expectations you have of them. At arm's length the frog orchid is one of the dullest flowers you could imagine. It looks about as interesting as the top few inches of a bolted spinach. But rarity has its own rewards – though they aren't always complimentary to the plant-hunter, I'm afraid. I don't know whether I'd misread the map and this was the place I should have been searching in the first place (or the map reference in the Flora had been slightly fudged, as it often is for rarer plants to keep the specimen hunters at bay), but I was a good 400 yards from the spot I had scanned originally. I felt decidedly prideful at the thought that I might have discovered a new site for the plant. All is vanity, I fear, when deliberate rarity hunting pays off. You feel as smugly accomplished as if you had simultaneously been rated 20/20 by an oculist and passed, with honours, an examination in field ecology.

But there are more creditable rewards to be had in finding a rarity. It does force you to look closely at the plant – to get your money's worth, I suppose. In close-up, and especially through a glass, the individual blooms of the frog orchid, of which a dozen are carried on short stalks at the top of the flower stalk, are fascinating constructions. They certainly merit the plant its name – and its equally reptilian Latin tag, *Coeloglossum* – though with their long dangling legs and over-large heads they look more like creatures out of Beatrix Potter than a textbook on amphibians.

The architecture of these blooms is principally designed to ensure that they are successfully pollinated. Small insects alight on the lip above the frog's legs and walk up it towards the spur which joins each flower to the stem. There is a ridge running along the centre that ensures that the insect keeps to one side or another of the lip. This causes its head to butt into the tiny pollen-bearing organ (the pollinium) that is situated at the mouth of the spur. This sticks to the insect and is carried off when it moves on to the next bloom. But it remains in an erect position for more than fifteen minutes, which is time enough for the insect to visit all the other blooms on a single plant and transfer to another spike. By then the pollinium will have drooped low enough for it to make contact with the stigma of another flower. These are sticky and snatch up pollen grains like flypaper as the insect moves about the new flower spike. It is a highly efficient fertilisation technique if there are enough insects about, and the orchid follows it up with a breakneck gestation period, ripening its seeds in as little as three or four weeks.

The frog orchid needs a reliable fertilisation and seeding process, for its roots very rarely survive more than a single flowering. This is happily not the case with a much commoner orchid, the spotted, whose tall pink catstail spikes were growing in the rough grass alongside one of the fairways. Although this species, like the frog orchid, takes four or five years between germination and first flowering, a single clump can produce flower spikes over many years. In addition the root will divide and gradually increase the number of shoots in the clump.

Sadly, the two finest spikes, both carrying over five inches of solid blooms, were lying on the ground – neatly severed by a niblick stroke, to judge from the closeness of the cut. The frog orchid should be thankful for its dull garb and secluded habits.

But the years of labour by all these orchids may be of no avail. As I write, plans are being drawn up to strike a motorway through the heart of this tiny oasis of downland. A road of this size will involve the ploughing up of a strip of soil hundreds of yards wide. In the face of devastations like this, neither express seed production nor duplicating roots could guarantee such fragile flowers' survival.

Gardens

Eighty per cent of British homes have gardens, 14 million assorted conglomerations of lawns, beds and hedges, which together occupy an area somewhat greater than the county of Dorset. They vary from the wild acres of the decaying country seat to the few square yards of terrace in the city centres. Yet for all that their uniformity is astonishing. I have never heard of a marsh being laid down in someone's garden or an artificial hill being raised. Yet other types of non-natural artefact proliferate: stone urns, lily ponds, double and triple flowered chrysanths, shrubs so delicate that they need weekly washes and injections and a room indoors for the winter.

The more closely you examine gardens the more mysterious their purpose becomes. At one level, of course, they are simply outdoor extensions of the house; pieces of personal territory that you can decorate as you please, and in which you can enjoy – as you do central heating and armchairs indoors – sun, air and privacy. Yet they are also plainly seen as pockets of condensed countryside. Gardens are above all places where things are *grown*. You would not feel comfortable calling the surroundings of a house that were utterly devoid of plants a garden. But the word is grown, not grow. It is the owner who feels he is in control over the unruliness of natural growth. He decides which living organisms shall be encouraged and which weeded out. And the patterns in which the chosen few are arranged are ones you would never find in the open countryside. Grass is grown in flat, shaven terraces, edges and borders cut square, flowers arranged in geometrical patterns and shrubs pruned back until they resemble household brushes. 'Tidiness' is the virtue most commonly sought after in gardens, sometimes with such enthusiasm that the fact that plants are living things seems almost incidental.

Yet suggest to most gardeners that they might achieve the order they are after more effectively, and with considerably less backache, if they replaced every living plant with a plastic replica, and they will be outraged. The yen to be not simply a dictator but a partner in a plant's growth, to be rewarded for hard and skilful husbandry, to experience a little of the unpredictables and seasonal changes of the natural work is, I think, lurking behind the clipped hedges of the fussiest gardener. I am sure that much of the excessive tidying that is apparent in gardens is more a result of social convention than deep-seated need. Rampant weeds in the vegetable patch or an unkempt shrubbery are, to some eyes, as sure signs of unneighbourliness or downright low morals as peeling paint. Two friends of mine who moved to a semi in a New Town in the North and allowed their front hedge to grow luxuriantly were visited during the night by the community vigilantes, who pruned back the offending bushes until they were the standard height for the street.

The lawn, which very few gardens are without, is a good instance. Convention decrees that the best lawns are those with the closest-cut and most uniform grass. Any other plants are black marks – despite the burnish of colour they give to the turf throughout the year, from the rash of speedwell blue in the spring to the rough purples of self-heal in the autumn. They are hounded with fork and weedkiller.

I have counted over twenty different species of wild flower (excluding grasses) on my lawn, many of them just those plants through which, in children's games, we have our first physical intimacy with nature: dandelion seed-heads for telling the time; daisies for chaplets; buttercups to shine under the chin; couch grass to wind into sister's hair as a Chinese Torture; ratstail plantains for guns; Lady's slipper and clovers to suck for nectar.

These flowers are part of children's lives precisely because they are weeds, abundant and resilient plants that grow comfortingly and accessibly close to us. If we drive them out of their domestic refuges into ghettoes in the deep countryside they will be driven out of what remains of our folk-lore as well. Lady's slipper – birdsfoot trefoil in the books – has over seventy different local names, including boxing gloves, butter-and-eggs, cuckoo's stockings, Devils' claws, fell bloom, grandmother's toenails, ground honeysuckle, kitty-two-shoes, milk maidens, pattens-and-clogs, rosy morn, Tom Thumb. It is an astonishing profusion of names for such a lowly plant, a record of fancies, superstitions, deep-felt beliefs and the sharp eyes and vividly functional vocabularies of our rural forebears. So the shoe-shaped, orange and egg-yolk yellow flowers became footwear, soft and fragrant enough for Our Lady – or for a cuckoo, if you were less pious. Later in the year the flowers transmute into pods, four or five black, birdlike claws – the Devil's fingers.

I would wager that half our popular names for plants originated out of the imaginations of children. It would be sad if urban children, cut off from the dandelion clocks and Tom Thumb's honeysuckles of the open countryside, were also robbed of them on their home patches by over-fastidious parents.

If wild flowers in a garden can be delight to children they are no less so to birds and insects. Nettles, for instance, can honestly be described as a blessed nuisance: they are the chief food plant of the caterpillars of three of the best-loved of all British butterflies – the red admiral, peacock and small tortoiseshell. A garden that has a small patch of nettles is that much more likely to be graced by the mature butterflies when they hatch in high summer.

If there are thistles too, it may be visited in autumn by a charm of goldfinches, flashing, spangled wings and xylophone trills amongst the thistledown. How much better these gaudy acrobats must look performing amongst the backgarden weeds than in the cages they were once caught for.

But it would be wrong to suggest that it is only wild flowers that attract wild creatures in the garden. Buddleia and sedum blossoms, for instance, are relished by butterflies, and many of the bright herbaceous annuals are great favourites with bees and other insects.

Insects are often defended because of the birds that are attracted to mop them up. I think this is a little unfair. Insects live intriguing, if rather obscure, lives of their own. Many are useful just going about their daily business. There would be no fruit crops if it weren't for the unquenchably sweet thirst of our bees; and twice as many greenfly if there were no ladybirds to eat them.

But I must confess that I've never really got to grips with the insect world. For me there are simply too many of them; myriads upon myriads of species distinguished from one another by factors as minute as an underwing tint or the number of segments in the body. And all this on a creature which may be no more than a sixteenth of an inch long! Not having a mind to kill them just to satisfy my colour-matching skills, I am forced to give up at this point, and look at the bugs for what they do, not for what they might be called. I suspect it is a salutary exercise.

And for insect-watching there is no better place than a deck-chair in a summer garden. The slightly drunk, hallucinatory feeling that comes from lying horizontal in the sun is a perfect state in which to nurture the short-sighted concentration needed for these tiny creatures. It was in such a near comatose sprawl that I first saw female ants pulling off their own wings – which are necessary for their ecstatically brief summer marriage flights but redundant in the underground nesting holes. It was here, too, I spotted a bee-fly, a laughably bottom-heavy creature, with a body as round and furry as an overripe cherry, yet only two wings to support it, and a needle-thin proboscis as long again as his body. It was hovering to sip the juices from a rose leaf. And once, whilst I was braving the sun in shorts, an unidentifiable fly began scaling the hairs on my leg. I must admit I was moved by its persistence. Neither puffing or shaking would move it. It hung on until it had chosen its own moment to leave. How does a creature as small and frail as this, so specialised in its demands, so orientated towards the present, ever find its way from a situation like that to a food plant which may be all of a mile away? I think we may be lucky that insects are too small and remote ever to have entered our understanding in the way that birds and flowers have. If we saw their lives for what they really are I think it might be too much for us to bear.

I fear I have already outraged most gardeners. This sort of sympathy should be reserved for the vegetables, not the wretched pests that gobble them to tatters. Well, it's undoubtedly true that there are as many insects that injure our cultivated plants as benefit them (though probably only a couple of hundred of our 20,000 species). But just as true that there are natural insecticides available in almost any garden at negligible cost. Try the accounts for a pair of great tits: a small quantity of fruit buds in the spring, and something like 10,000 grubs a month during the breeding season. Three and half inches of wren – a bird which scarcely ever demeans itself with vegetarian food – can absorb 500 caterpillars and aphids a day.

A gardener who wants to contain his insects can therefore do worse than invest in a few pairs of insectivorous birds. He won't need to allow his garden to revert to wild forest to do this. There are plenty of birds which are quite happy to set up house in the ornamental shrubs which are the nearest approximation to hedges and woods you find in most gardens.

When I lived in the suburbs, our garden, plus the two adjoining, could claim in a normal year the following breeding birds: a pair of linnets in a forsythia bush barely six feet high; greenfinches at the top of a fir; willow warblers at the base of a clump of michaelmas daisies. Our transplanted Christmas tree (about eight years old) was a double-storey dwelling for blackbirds and thrushes, whose nests were barely three feet apart. In an assortment of different strains of cypress, about thirty trees in all, were two pairs of dunnock, three blackbirds, and one song thrush. And one pair each of great tit and blue in nesting boxes. That I think was the total nest quota for the three gardens. Notice that not one of them was in a native British shrub.

And if town birds are adaptable in their choice of breeding sites, they are equally so in their choice of nest material, being as resourceful in their scrounging as any dustbin-picker. Pound notes, corrugated paper and chewed-up polythene bags have all been found in garden nests. Crow and pigeon nests in industrial areas have been found woven entirely out of strands of wire. One pair of collared doves in Jersey, obviously determined to move with the times, built a wire nest on top of a lagged steam pipe in a chemical works. Our blue tits (that also learned to bathe in the lawn spray) were more conventional, if no less inventive. They lined their nest with hairs yanked out of our cat's dried-out fur-balls. Not that blue tits always have it their own way in the nest-building stakes. One was watched being pinned down by a pair of sparrows, which were sadistically pulling out its breast feathers and ferrying them back to their drain-pipe nest.

But the most adaptable of all garden birds is without doubt the blackbird, now Britain's commonest bird and twice as common in urban and suburban areas as in the open countryside. Originally a bird of the copses and hedgerows of the old-style farming landscape, it has this century spread steadily inwards towards built-up zones, first into parks and the well-wooded gardens of the suburbs, and eventually into the heart of the towns themselves. Now there is scarcely anywhere a patch of ground with a modicum of greenery that does not support a resident pair.

One can only speculate on the reasons behind the colossal success of the blackbird in adapting to new environments over the last fifty years. It has involved not only an increasing willingness to tolerate men, but great flexibility in the choice of food and nesting sites. Was there some sort of population explosion amongst blackbirds, causing them to prospect for *lebensraum* in ever more diverse surroundings? Or did a new strain of hardy and adaptable birds develop, enabling the population to grow and spread more gradually?

If it's impossible to pinpoint precisely why the spread occurred we can trace how, in practical terms, it has been achieved. Firstly, the blackbird has become almost totally omnivorous. Unlike its cousin the song thrush, whose diet is three quarters flesh, the blackbird is more than eighty per cent vegetarian in the urban areas. His diet is a hotch-potch of fruit, flower petals, insects and bread and fat thrown out by householders. Blackbirds have even been observed fishing for newts from the lily pads in suburban ponds.

Once a species has learned to tolerate the presence of man he is plainly going to have an easier time, not just because of the additional food sources opened up to him, but because a whole new range of nesting territories become available. Blackbirds traditionally nest a few feet up in a bush or tangle of ivy. Yet in urban areas they seem equally happy in holes in walls or on the bend of a rainwater pipe. We understand so little about what a bird needs from a nesting site. What induces a blackbird to choose sites like these when there are often seemingly perfect bushes only yards away? What sort of supernatural tolerance and flexibility was possessed by that handful of blackbirds which have been recorded nesting in the boots of cars, sitting steadfast on their eggs whilst their mobile homes were trundled back and forth to work, and nonchalantly disembarking to feed when the commuting was over?

n the time it to draw this
has taken me to draw this
the shadows will have moved right round
the shadows will have moved
.and the sun will have finished its cou

PART THREE

Autumn: Moving On

AUTUMN, IN THE NATURAL WORLD, is the time for passing on. Migrant birds which have raised their young during our few uncertain months of summer warmth move away to winter in the tropics. Others, passing from the far north to the same off-season resorts, pause here to replenish the energy burnt up on their marathon flights. Flowers fade and go to seed. And these migrate too, on the wind and the fur of animals, and – because man is a migratory creature as well – in shoes and the slipstream of trains. Above all autumn is a time of decay, when the remains of plants and animals that have not survived the population explosion of the breeding season begin to be broken down by the multitude of small organisms in the soil. Worms, insects, bacteria, and the moulds and fungi that flourish in the mild, damp climate of this season are all involved in turning these dead remains into the food supply for the next generation in the spring. It is one of the key links in the ecological cycle, this thriving of life on decay. Unless there were ways in which the remains and waste products of living organisms could be returned to the earth and broken down into their constituent organic and mineral chemicals, life as we know it would come to a halt. There would be no soil, just sterile ground sucked dry of its food resources and choked under the luxuriant but useless piles of corpses in which these were trapped.

Urban humans, finding the processes of decay and excretion distasteful (and more understandably, unhygienic) has chosen to remove his own waste products out of sight and out of smell. The disposal of human refuse happens largely on the perimeters of towns and cities, in that no-man's-land of rubbish tips and sewage farms. In the fall, by a happy coincidence of all manner of passings-on, these places become the scenes of great flurries of biological activity.

The expression 'fall' could equally well be derived from birds as from leaves, as this is the season when migrants drop down for rest and food during their long flights south. Sewage farms are one of the most popular inland stopping-off points. Yet it was not until the early years of this century that bird-watchers began to turn their glasses on to these farms. They found huge flocks of common resident birds feeding and nesting in the rough weeds at the edge of the farms, but most excitingly, rare and elegant marshland waders stopping off to feed on the beds themselves.

To understand why birds whose natural winter homes are wild and lonely estuaries should be attracted to these insalubrious patches of sludge, often only hundreds of yards from the factory belt, we have to look at the mechanics of the old-style farms. These can be as varied in detail as the habitats they subsequently produce; but the most basic system of purification involves the pumping of liquefied sewage into large pools dug out of the ground or enclosed between artificially earthed-up banks. These pools act as settling beds for the sludge. As they silt up the water is drained off, purified and returned to the river system. The pools thus slowly dry out, and are eventually either ploughed up and sown with a crop, or dug out for use as manure. For the whole of this cycle the sludge itself abounds with worms and insects.

Over a period of time the beds provide a range of habitats that are almost identical to those you would find around an estuary or salt-marsh, from the early months (or after a rainy spell) when the beds may be completely under water, through a stage when there is exposed mud, lagoons, and a fringe of annual weeds, to the final hard-baked mud and rough herbage.

And those birds that are called waders precisely because of their perfect adaptation to sloshing about and feeding in mud, aren't slow to notice the similarities in the terrain and the pickings. For a bird migrating between Africa and the northern European moors and tundra, these artificial inland marshes are ideal service stations.

The farm I visited most often that September was one of the last of the large sludge settling beds still operating in this country. It is not far short of half a mile square and lies at the mouth of a V formed by two runways at the western edge of Heathrow Airport. More importantly, from a migrant bird's-eye-view, it's near the centre of that vast cone of water that widens out down the River Colne towards the Thames valley. No one knows with any certainty the precise routes migrating birds take through this country, or indeed, if there are any standard routes. But there is little doubt that they do follow chains of landmarks, and that water birds in particular flight along waterway systems that can both guide them and feed them. Many of the southbound waders follow the line of the East coast with its chain of low-lying marshes. Others, depending on weather, wind and factors as imponderable as their own travelling experience, may strike inland at the Wash, say, and continuing in a southerly direction through the Fens, alight on this skein of artificial water, with its mud-fringed gravel pits and secluded sewage farms.

Whichever way they came I knew that this expanse of sludge had a reputation for drawing in rare and exotic globetrotters as surely as a fashionable restaurant. But on my first two visits I saw not a single wading bird. Perhaps I had picked bad times. They were both days in early September, hot windless afternoons. Not the sort of conditions in which migrants like to move about much. But I suspect they were there all right, resting up in the shaded edges of the pools, waiting for the night and maybe a touch of following wind. And my surroundings were hardly those to encourage single-minded searchings for obscure brown shapes roosting under the grassy overhangs. The jets throbbed over at least once a minute. The smell, though by no means nauseating, was too strong to ignore. The sheer look of the place was enough to make one gape. The pools to the west, some of them hundreds of yards wide, were shored-up and criss-crossed by banks – something like the sea-walls built to hold back the flood-tides in coastal areas. And a horrendous flood there could well have been if one of these banks broke. Fresh sludge was being continuously pumped into the wettest pools, making their surface look like some ghastly hot spring. I eyed the red notices, saying WARNING: 20 FEET DEEP, and kept well to the centre of the paths as I worked round the farm.

There was plenty to make up for my failure to find any waders. The banks were as lush with vegetation as you could expect for the surrounds of what was virtually a giant manure heap. Tomatoes had been carried here as seeds wrapped up in their own fertiliser (a little like those new-fangled 'pelleted' seeds) and were already ripening in the Indian summer. The seed-bearing weeds, fat hen, clovers, docks and thistles, were busy with drifts of reed buntings, linnets, sky-larks, and best of all, tree-sparrows. I have never met a bird-watcher who hasn't a soft spot for the tree-sparrow. I think perhaps it's the unexpectedness of a dapper chestnut cap and black cheek dimples on a bird that otherwise looks so much like an ordinary spadger that is so pleasing.

Martins and swallows were hawking over the beds. Twice I saw a weasel lope across the perimeter road, no doubt after the same prey as the kestrels that were forever in the air. And gyrating round a boggy stream between the settling beds were two demoiselle flies. I was saddened later to discover that someone had given these the graceless name of 'banded agrions'. They deserve something better for their astonishing translucent wings, stuck out like the arms of a windmill and each adorned with a surprising black beauty spot.

When I went back to the farm a fortnight later the portents were altogether better. It was early evening and there was a light wind getting up from the East. As I bussed down towards the farm I was pleased to see that one small natural cycle was being completed, and that sewage sludge was being sprayed back on to the nearby market garden fields. And just as I arrived at the farm a flock of five ruffs dashed overhead, jinking and twisting down on to one of the far beds. It was going to be a good evening.

In spite of the din, I felt I ought to observe some of the niceties of birding. I went down on my stomach and crept slowly up the bank towards the two wet beds that usually attract the best birds. I scoured them with my binoculars, and there was a flock of about sixty lapwing feeding restlessly in a far corner. They were rising and settling again on their slow wings like windblown newspaper. But no waders.

I got up onto the path that runs along the top of the banks and began walking across the farm. After about a quarter of a mile a wader shot out of a foul-looking ditch to my right, brilliant white rump glaring against dark body and sharp wings. It towered up, flying rapidly and jerkily like a snipe, giving a ringing *weet-tluitt-tluitt* call. It was a green sandpiper, close relation of the common sandpiper I had seen in the spring, moving down from its nesting grounds in north-eastern Europe. I followed it through my glasses as it zig-zagged off, still calling, high into the west. As I panned down to the pools I'd first looked at I could see that there was now a scattering of birds feeding on them. I hurried back and settled down on the bank for a spot of what that maverick Scots ornithologist Desmond Nethersole-Thompson has nicknamed 'arsing'.

What lay in front of me now was as extraordinary and contradictory a panorama as I think I've ever seen. Dusk was closing in, and but for the string of neon lamps in the distance, I could have been on an estuary at low-tide. Although the light was failing, waders seemed to be appearing from nowhere, limbering up for the next leg of their migration flights through the night skies. On the pool to my right a few dunlin with their toothpick bills were scuttling about like mice. A common sandpiper bobbed on a tussocky island.

But it was the bed directly in front of me that was making my eyes goggle. Right in the centre was a tall and delicate wader picking his way among the puddles. It was too dark to tell for certain what he was at this distance, and so for a while I was forced to look at him simply as a bird. In silhouette he became a working model of how perfectly waders are adapted to their muddy habitats: the thin bill for winkling out insects below the surface; the dancer's legs, long, flexible, set well back for balance, picked fastidiously out of the sludge at each step; the lean of body forward and the stretched neck, tilting the bill down towards the mud.

Then suddenly he was up, towering away to the west like the sandpiper. The shadow play was over. He was a real flesh and feathers bird again, about his urgent and arduous business. And able to see what he was at last I was delighted to tick off a rarity. For there was no mistaking that white V-shaped rump and shrill chirrup, like a porter hailing a taxi. It was a dusky redshank, one of the scarcest waders to regularly visit this farm. Only a handful are seen every autumn on their long flights from inside the Arctic circle to the Mediterranean.

It is extraordinary, the charge that seeing even a drab rarity can give you. I think it is partly the sense of privilege at having crossed paths with one of these solitary vagrants. It is literally a unique experience. You rarely know when the bird arrived or how long it will stay. As like as not it will be gone if you come looking for it again.

And providentially, as this lean wader vanished into the gloom, there lumbered up behind it another of the relentless stream of jetliners, bound perhaps for the same destination. They made a glib and obvious symbol, this pair, but one impossible to ignore: the brutish, ear-splitting airliner, burning tons of our dwindling energy resources and spewing its exhaust residue in a sticky film not only over all the plant life in the area, but even, cannibalistically, over other ground-based vehicles; and this swift 12-inch-long bird, whose night-flight noise has caused no more disturbance than to make a few sharp-eared ornithologists nostalgic for lonelier places. There are waders that come to this farm on rare occasions – Baird's, buff-breasted and pectoral sandpipers – that have been blown by Westerly gales off migration flights intended to take them between Alaska and South America. They weigh no more than a few ounces, yet they have made the 3,000-mile transatlantic crossing without a single refuelling stop.

It is impossible to describe the noise that a jet makes on take-off to someone who hasn't stayed for a while on the edge of an airport. It can't really be called a roar, for that implies something altogether too steady and consistent. Your eardrums are so assaulted by the vibrations that for split seconds they seem to go into a state of protective anaesthesia. So that what you hear is more like crackle, rising and falling in waves as the plane passes over. I was amazed (and slightly disappointed) on my visits to the farm at just how little concern the birds showed at this clamour above them. Not once did I see a bird take flight obviously as a result of jet noise (in the way they invariably do at a sonic boom, that on a coastal marsh can spill more panic-stricken birds into the air than you ever dreamt were about).

A week later, on an early morning visit, I was able to watch the reactions of a small flock of mixed waders at very close quarters and under perfect light. Most would stop feeding when an especially thunderous machine went overhead, and would cower down close to the sludge. There was a special touch of pathos in one of the groups of birds: a little stint, our smallest wader and no larger than a robin, hunched like a chick against the legs of a magisterial ruff, three times his size.

It is striking how much birds of different species stick together on migration, as if they were looking for company and security on their long and hazardous flights. A few weeks earlier, on a reservoir a few miles away, I had seen a black tern and a juvenile little gull wafting together in tandem over the surface of the water. These species have little more in common than superficial similarities in shape, flight style, and breeding grounds. Yet these two birds were flying together as intimately as mother and child, so much so that at a distance I thought this was what they were. It was almost as if they were joined by long elastic. The young gull would not let the adult tern pull out more than forty or so yards in front before it scooted back behind.

But this was nothing to the sociability I saw this morning. A group of five waders of four different species – two dunlin, one little stint, a ringed plover and a ruff – were skitting about the settling beds as tightly as any single species flock, taking off and manoeuvring in what, to the human eye, was perfect unison.

And it was a similar display that was my last sight that darkening evening after the dusky redshank had left. A little stint dodging nervously about with two stocky ringed plovers, never straying more than a few feet from them or failing to fly when they flew. I think I came nearer at that moment, sprawled improbably on a sewage farm bank, to understanding what I had been looking at all that year. We were all just going home, this motley collection of birds and I, finding what refreshment we could in the makeshift landscapes on our way, ignoring for a moment those rigid categories by which biologists break up the natural world, in the common business of keeping body and soul together.

Rubbish tips, I suppose, are the real untouchables in our caste system of landscapes. They are ugly, smelly, and act like magnifying glasses to the swelling volume of indestructible garbage that we toss over our shoulders. But nature, always more economically efficient than us, does what it can to make use of these places, and what sewage farms are to birds, refuse tips are to plants.

This is not really the place to look into the complex technology and increasingly involved ethics of rubbish disposal. Within the next decade or so the haphazard dumping of refuse on tips is likely to become an indulgence we can afford neither in terms of the ground space it occupies nor the resources it squanders. Already some local authorities are developing techniques for extracting valuable elements (particularly metals) from garbage and incinerating as much as possible of the remainder, using the precious calories generated for community heating schemes. There's no doubt that systems of this sort will become more widespread, and that the old-style rubbish tip will become a museum-piece, a habitat as rare and relict as a fen. (It would be ironic if the last few examples of a land-use that many amenity societies are fighting to eradicate ended up as nature reserves, artificially conserved in all their fertile slumminess!) This is the fate of land in the unofficial countryside. This year's wasteland is next year's wasted land.

But for the time being, most of our household refuse, and a fair amount of non-toxic industrial waste, will continue simply to be dumped on specially assigned plots of ground at the edges of towns. Sometimes the designated area is an abandoned quarry or gravel pit. More often it's a patch of low-lying waste ground with little obvious potential for farming or housing. But whatever the chosen receptacle, the technique of disposal follows much the same pattern. The garbage – kitchen and garden refuse that will eventually decay, plastic containers that won't, ash, glass, a multitude of small solid objects from thrown-out toys to motor car tyres, the waste from tanneries and mills, the whole adding up to nearly 10 cwt. per person per year – is tipped from the carts and strewn in a thin layer across a section of the tip. Some of the paper and more easily combustible materials may be roughly sorted out for burning, and the rest covered by bulldozer with a thin layer of soil. This may come from another part of the dump or be imported from nearby earthworks. This plot is then allowed to settle for a few months before another stratum of refuse is laid over it.

Consider then the geology of the surface of a tip from a plant's point of view. On the top, a thin layer of well-worked soil. Underneath, what amounts to a layer of vegetable manure, slowly rotting as the bacteria and fungi get their teeth into it. The drainage and aeration are good on account of the loose packing of the vegetable refuse and its skeleton of solid debris. There is light, for there's no time for any shade-giving shrubs to become established, and even warmth from the decaying vegetable matter. In short, the dump is like nothing so much as a huge compost heap, and is mightily congenial to plant growth. The snag is the bulldozers and the ominous looming of the next smothering layer of garbage. So it is the fast growing annuals, those opportunist weeds that are so adept at nipping into bare and short-lived plots of ground, that make out best here. The bulk of the flowers are those that you would find in any patch of disturbed ground – groundsel, petty spurge, fat hen, shepherd's purse, docks. There will also be a smattering of those low-lying plants that are tolerant of the constant pounding of the dustcarts: plantains, knotgrass and pineapple weed. And there are perennial plants that actually thrive from being sliced up by the bulldozers, like the common creeping thistle, which can send up new shoots from strips of chopped-up root.

But if rubbish tips nourished these plants alone, they'd warrant no more special attention than any other type of waste ground. It is the plant material – and seeds in particular – that finds its way into the ground as part of the refuse itself that can turn dumps into such exciting hunting grounds. And it is the unnatural origins of this plant material that is responsible for the excitement.

Even ordinary kitchen refuse can provide the beginnings of a huge range of plants. There may be discarded but still fertile root vegetables, the remains of bottles of oriental spice, the sweepings from the budgie's cage. And it is not just that, cosseted in the well-prepared refuse beds, these can turn into flowers that are an astonishment to find blooming in a down-and-out English field, but that each crop is fascinatingly tied to the social changes in the community that threw out the refuse. A newly-settled immigrant group may bring in their native spices with them. A local firm's latest import line can introduce seeds from halfway across the world, caught up in the packaging materials. Even an ephemeral fad for a new vegetable will show up eventually in the tip flora.

It's typical of botanising in the unofficial countryside that your techniques can turn out to be as eccentric as your quarry. It didn't seem incongruous that my first encounter with the flora of refuse dumps was on a charabanc tour of the East London tips on a dull day at the tail-end of September. My travelling companions were for the most part professional botanists – which was lucky for me, for the plants we discovered that day were a stunning and exotic collection that I would have been hard pressed to sort out from my humble collection of field guides.

Most of London's rubbish is dumped on the rough marshes that lie on both sides of the Thames estuary, and it was on one of these in South Essex that we began our forage. It's not an encouraging prospect, the first sight of one of these really big dumps. They are wreathed perpetually by hazy smoke and permeated by an unmistakable musty smell of ash mixed with decaying vegetables. Yet they have a rural character – marshland crossed with working farmyard perhaps – that is often quite absent from our pampered city parks.

This particular tip was a showpiece for bird-seed flowers. The oily seeds that are sold as food for cage birds are imported in prodigious quantities from all over the world (together with seeds of the local weeds). Thirteen thousand tons of canary grass seed alone are brought in every year. Much of this is spilled inside the cages and ends up – ready-fertilised with a dressing of bird droppings – on the tips.

Here, the sunflowers, products of the plumpest and most favoured seeds, outshone everything else, awkward though they looked thrusting out of this flat and derelict moor. Then there were the deep purple cascades of love-lies-bleeding; countless breeds of millet and canary grass from Australia, Morocco and South America; niger from India; yellow safflowers, blue flaxes, and most curious of all, a shoo-fly plant from Peru, with pale lilac flowers tightly closed in the gloom and Chinese lantern fruit cases.

These were the brightest and most conspicuous flowers on the dump. But a plant doesn't need to have a gaudy blossom to ensure its discovery in these places. Most are growing against a back-cloth of bare soil, not a camouflage of thick grass. And grubbing about with your eyes fixed firmly on the ground is not simply a matter of scientific self-discipline but of sheer survival among the broken bottles and wrecked prams.

So we chanced upon many meek and sombre plants, but very few that hadn't a fascinating history to compensate for their drab looks. One of the very first plants I found myself on this ramble was another thorn-apple, perhaps sprung up from drug manufacturer's refuse. This was almost certainly the origin of the deadly nightshade plant growing only a hundred yards away, climbing mangily amongst the clutter, and already bearing its seductive black cherries. In the wild, deadly nightshade grows almost exclusively on chalk and limestone. But it is still cultivated in this country for the drug *belladonna*, which is a valuable local anaesthetic, particularly in eye surgery. It's pleasing that the plant should be used in this way under its Latin name, for it echoes the practice of the old herbalists. By all accounts the plant acquired its name in Italy, where it was called *herba bella donna* (beautiful lady herb), since the juice of the leaves was used as a cosmetic to give an alluring dilation to the pupil of the eye. It must have been a scary business, for the whole plant is so toxic (children have been killed by as few as three berries), that it was not until the nineteenth century that chemists could administer it internally with safety.

A plant with an even more curious pharmacological effect was buckwheat, the source of those splendid pancakes that are served in drug-stores across America. These are made from the nutritious seeds, ground up into flour. But if the green parts of the plant are eaten by animals with pale skins (including man), they are apt to develop 'fagopyrism' – a form of photosensitivity which results in the animals developing allergic rashes if they're exposed to strong light. Buckwheat probably came to this country from Asia in the fifteenth or sixteenth century, and up until the nineteenth was widely grown for chicken-feed and as a subsistence cereal crop for humans. The early settlers took it to America with them, and it grew readily in the poor soils of New England. It is this tolerance of rough ground and rapid growth that makes buckwheat such a regular denizen of the dumps. Yet it's a shame that it's confined to these waste places. Buckwheat cakes would taste as good over here as they do in America, where the plant is still regarded as a commercially viable crop. But even forgetting its food value, it's a compact and attractive little plant, with its triangular spinach-green leaves and pyramidal seeds. A field of buckwheat in flower must have been a marvellously mottled thing, the spikes of white blossoms against the rich green, shot through with the red-brown of the stalks.

It was a positive witches' garden, this tip. To complete a potent trio there was a single plant of darnel rye-grass, in all probability the 'tares' of the Bible. Darnel was a rampant weed of arable land in Elizabethan times, and not one that farmers could turn a blind eye to, literally: bread containing its seeds as impurities could blur the sight and cause convulsions. Modern grain screening techniques can filter out darnel's fruits, which are only two-thirds the width of wheat ears, and the grass is consequently almost extinct as an agricultural weed. But seeds still find their way into this country as impurities in bird-seed crops.

Virgil mentions darnel in *The Georgics*. Shakespeare moans about the taste of bread containing it. John Donne quotes the legend that slipshod husbandry made wholesome wheat turn into this poisonous weed (called cockle then):

> Good seed degenerates, and oft obeys
> The soil's disease, and into Cockle strays.

Two thousand years of agricultural and mythological history in this one weed. No wonder the botanists became excited when one of these ancient plants was found. There was a delightful ritual that accompanied these special discoveries. The expedition leader would blow a whistle, and the members of the party leave their private explorations and cluster round the plant. Photos would be taken, and a debate begin about who should 'carry on' the plant. All these flowers would be smothered anyway within the next few weeks, so for once it was excusable to dig them up and carry them back to greenhouses and botanical gardens, to nurse them through to seed-time or next flowering. What astonishing herbaceous beds some of these botanists must have. And what frustrated yearnings to gather bushels of wild flowers too, to judge from the great polythene bagfuls of cuttings and blossoms that were gleefully humped back to the coach!

Back on board we sifted through our findings. By the time we had reached our next stop – a dump behind the Ford factory at Dagenham – the warmth inside the coach had made those secretive shoo-fly blossoms open wide.

We had moved farther downriver, and passed brackish ditches where giant hogweed and sea aster grew equally side by side. It was private land here, and we poked about the dump watched by a handful of bemused security guards. They needn't have worried. It was not the factory and its encircling acres of unregistered cars that we had our eyes on, but the ash raked out of its furnaces and spread over this waste ground. In this apparently sterile refuse a large colony of Russian thistle had established itself. This native of arid soils in Eurasia has been spreading across the world, homing in, as immigrant plants uncannily will, on patches of ground that resemble its natural habitat. It's not a particularly distinguished plant, looking a little like a low-lying gorse. But we know it better than we think: remember those balls of tumble-weed that roll around the dusty plain in cowboy films? They are Russian thistle. Those mobile, self-uprooted clumps are the plant's specialised technique for distribution in inhospitable terrain. They are blown about until they stick on a patch of ground sufficiently fertile for them to take root. Russian thistle is spreading, and maybe one dust-blown evening, the drinkers in Dagenham saloons will look out into the main street to see the tumbleweeds rolling past their reined-up Cortinas.

Not, perhaps, a particularly useful employment for the refuse of one of our most wasteful industries. But the success of recycling is in the eye of the beholder!

Every tip seemed to have its specialist leanings. Over the river and farther east still, we visited a veritable spice garden. Cumin, fenugreek, coriander, dill, fennel – you could have flavoured a whole Indian meal from this one dump. These could well have been restaurant throw-outs, though the ancient oriental spice ajowan (*Trachyspermum ammi*), that we also discovered, had more likely found its way here in bird-seed. Ajowan is an inconspicuous little umbelliferate and caused some difficulty to the less experienced members of our party. But not to the gang of young totters that latched onto us at this tip. They were spending their Saturday afternoon ferreting for rather more substantial trophies than we were, and were clearly astonished at the spectacle of this gaggle of donnish strangers picking over the weeds on their manor.

They followed us round besieging us with questions, and yanking up plants for identification. After a while they fanned out by themselves, gathering up specimens which they channelled back to us through their gang leader. One of the younger children poked an ajowan under the nose of this burgeoning taxonomist. 'Ammy', he said in best Cockney Latin. 'Nah, they've had that already.' I wish some of our educational cynics could have seen these nine-year-old East End kids getting to grips with one of our most difficult plant families – and some botanical Latin to boot – in thirty minutes flat.

This was the dump, too, where we found the biggest marijuana plant (*Cannabis sativa*), that I have ever seen, five feet tall and nearly as wide. Until the drug scare began, hemp seeds were a regular ingredient of most proprietary bird foods. Now the seed wholesalers will indignantly deny that any smuggle themselves through the new screening techniques. But a few always do, and are liable to spring to life anywhere. If this should happen to be in the garden of a wild bird fancier, he may have a tricky job explaining to a sharp-eyed constable – drilled in identification but not in the mitigating enterprise of alien weed seeds – that he is not farming the stuff.

Eyeing this magnificent, lupin-leaved clump, whose flowering tops would contain only a fraction of the active drug compared to those ripened in hotter climates, but which could still fetch a pound or two on the black market, I wondered how the Greater London Council would get off the hook if they were busted for growing the plant on their property!

It was the last tip that was my personal favourite, tucked under a loop of the Thames about fifteen miles east of St Paul's. Looking across it we could see flocks of brent geese flighting downriver, and the tops of the barges that are used as another way of ferrying refuse out of the city.

It was not until we reached this dump, late in the afternoon, that I discovered the source of the monotonous chirping that had been a constant background to our meanderings that day. It was the crickets that were clustered in dozens underneath the vegetation. The common house cricket was the most abundant, but there were at least two other species, which could well have come here along with the garbage they feed on. Crickets and cockroaches from the tropics are often found in tips which receive refuse from dockside areas.

There were more functional growths here to add to those bulging polythene bags. Water melons, pumpkins, tomatoes that had ripened up in the Indian summer, and gourds knobbly enough to grace any Swedish fruit bowl. It's a measure of just how much the jungle-like luxuriance of these places infects one, that I found myself tweaking plastic chrysanthemums and rubber balls just to make sure they weren't living!

It had been an extraordinary day, and one to whip up the appetite, for all the stifling air. Stopping off for a celebratory curry on the way home, I took pot luck with a dish with the temptingly evocative name of 'green gram'. It was a delightful, but, I felt, wholly suitable coincidence, that it turned out to be none other than mung bean, the last plant we had found on that self-made market garden south of the river.

There are botanists who turn up their noses at these alien plants – and not just because of the miasmic air that so often surrounds them. They aren't British, they say. They flourish one year and clear out the next.

I think these purists tend to forget that much of our flora is recently arrived, and that even flowers as apparently solidly English as the poppy are immigrants introduced by early colonists. And though some of these casual immigrants may be unwelcome in the countryside, where they can oust the more traditional flowers,

they surely have a place in the cosmopolitan and transient culture
of a city. I find the distaste for them intolerant and academic. It is
also illogical, as one of our most human botanical writers, David
McClintock, has pointed out:

> The lesson, as I see it, of Buxbaum's Speedwell, Sycamore,
> Cut-leaved Self-heal and Dragon's Teeth – and of various
> other similar plants – is that it is often hard without
> historical evidence to be sure whether any plant is native
> or not. Our flora is, as we have said, always changing in
> response to climate, man and other factors, some no doubt
> unappreciated or under-appreciated by us. In many books,
> plants get catalogued as natives, denizens, colonists, aliens,
> casuals, etc. – these are actually the terms used by H. C.
> Watson and much favoured since; and there are certainly
> advantages in thus attempting to assess status. But it does
> also lead to snobbery and exclusiveness, for any but the first
> of these categories was looked down on by most people –
> 'Oh, just an alien', and therefore not worth naming even;
> or if it was named, it would be relegated to an appendix
> or small type. This attitude still lingers among some
> professionals, and valuable records have been thereby lost.
> Why, except in the recent 'Flora of South Lancs', Sycamores
> are invariably, even after two-thirds of a millennium,
> branded as aliens. And yet what would these same people
> say if I retorted that they were not English because their
> ancestors had only come over with the Conqueror? There
> have been many fewer generations of men since 1066 than of
> Buxbaum's Speedwell since 1825.
>
> *Companion to Flowers,* 1966

The wild flowers of our towns and cities would be a drab lot if it
weren't for these immigrants. For as I've tried to show, they're not
only fascinating echoes of the human life in urban areas, but a vastly
colourful collection. Buddleia – which, believe it or not, arrived as

a garden shrub from China as late as 1896 – has escaped to give a splash of lilac brilliance to the most unpromising railway sidings. Brass buttons, from South America, spiny cocklebur thistle and a curious bur-marigold called *Bidens pilosa*, came over as seeds caught up in imported wool fleeces. Oxford ragwort, which grows naturally on volcanic ash near Mount Etna, escaped from the Botanic Gardens at Oxford in the nineteenth century, and migrating up the railway tracks found an equally congenial home amongst the burnt-out rubble of war-time London. Prospecting amongst these bomb-sites, one botanist discovered a Chinese apricot shrub, which he fancifully – but I think quite justifiably – guessed had sprung from a fruit-stone thrown away by a sailor on leave from Hong Kong. I found an American evening primrose, with its beautiful pale yellow peony-like flowers, in full flower at the edge of a building site. And, near that hop-draped hemlock, a network of everlasting pea, a naturalised garden escape from the Near East.

Everlasting pea also flourishes along the railway embankments, its garish magenta flowers unmistakable even from a fast-moving train. And here, too, you will see Japanese knotweed, so fast growing and expansive that it is the one immigrant that it is reasonable to be a little nervous about. Yet it's not without its own charms. Its fat shoots look like some fairground asparagus, with their mottled shafts and scarlet leaf scales, and taste almost as good.

Railways appear time and time again in the biographies of immigrant plants. Their fertile embankments form an interlocking network of green lanes along which plants can spread, from seaport to farmland. The trains themselves can act as carriers for seeds, either ferrying them physically or sucking them along in their slipstream. Goods sidings are one of the richest sites for immigrant flowers – and not just 'foreign' immigrants, either. Seaside plants like wall-pepper, wild antirrhinum and wallflower, will settle down in the shingle-like ballast between inland tracks. When there were steam trains, scarce ferns used to sprout out of the moist brickwork near stations and tunnels. Sometimes these ferns were hundreds of miles out of their usual range, emigrating as spores on the locomotives.

But it would be wrong to see railways as benefiting only immigrant plants. They are also amongst the finest sites for our native wild flowers. The embankments (especially the south-facing ones, which pick up more sun and warmth per square inch) are well-lit and well-drained and are safer even than a nature reserve from all but the most reckless pickers. And though British Rail don't seem to be interested in the look of their embankments (in the way that, for instance, the Department of the Environment is concerned about motorway verges) they use a gentle touch when it comes to management.

But the embankment flowers are an amenity – especially on a commuter journey to work. It can be a neck-cricking business trying to spot individual species from an express, but the seclusion of the embankments has meant that colonies can build up, and you can enjoy the masses of colour that result. You can witness the whole procession of colour and bulk of England's wild flowers on a year's travelling: the pale, low-lying flowers of the spring – primroses, wild strawberries, cowslips; the brighter poppies, St John's worts and the knapweeds, flowering taller as the grass grows about them, through to the thick and glorious clumps of rosebay and golden rod in high summer.

Richard Jefferies, prophetic as always, saw in the 1870s the sanctuary that the railways would provide for our flora:

> Driven from the fields by plough and hoe, cast out from
> the pleasure-grounds of modern houses, pulled up and
> hurled over the wall to wither as accursed things, they
> have taken refuge on the embankment and cutting.
>   There they can flourish and ripen their seed, little
> harassed even by the scythe and never by grazing cattle. So
> it happens that, extremes meeting, the wild-flower, with its

old-world associations, often grows most freely within a few feet of the wheels of the locomotive. Purple heathbells gleam from shrub-like bunches dotted along the slope; purple knapweeds lower down in the grass; blue scabious, yellow hawkweeds where the soil is thinner and harebells on the very summit; these are but a few upon which the eye lights while gliding by.

Nature Near London, 1879

PART FOUR

Winter: Survival

IT WAS LATE NOVEMBER, time for action to prepare for the approaching cold. The little stints had side-stepped the problem by getting away from it all. If they had survived the 4,000-mile journey they would by now be basking in the sand and sun of the southern African river deltas. The great crested grebes had dropped their extravagant breeding season plumage, and the territorial jealousies that go with it. They were beginning to crowd together on the gravel pits. Thistle roots would be threading their way towards as yet uncolonised patches of subsoil. Seeds, their wanderings over, would be conserving their food supplies until the next warm spell. To judge from the quantity I had brushed off my trousers with a new interest over the year, from the pin-heads of enchanter's nightshade to the bristly marbles of burdock, I had been used as an unwitting carrier by a dozen different species.

But there was one plant for which I'd been a more willing helper. That gravel-pit thorn-apple had survived to produce an abundance of its spiky fruits. To make up for that episode of wanton destruction in a Hampshire station, I had gathered a couple of them in October and broadcast their seeds out of harm's way – but not out of sight – behind the tall railings of an electricity substation.

There had been changes in the habitats, too. The old watercress beds where the grey wagtails had nested were being excavated for a fishing mere. Most of the bankside vegetation had been destroyed and the only birds likely to make a living there for the next year or two would be the wintering lapwings and gulls which were already arriving in force.

The long hot autumn had lasted until the middle of the month. There had been no more than an inch or so of rain since August, and when I walked along the canal at the end of November, the water level in the cut and its feeder stream were still a foot below their normal tidemark. In places this stream was little more than a muddy gutter, and under a willow tree I was able to watch a snipe feeding. It was not only up to its knees in the ooze but up to its eyes as well; all two-and-a-half inches of its flexibly tipped bill were buried under the mud.

The towpath hedges looked as anaemic as the water. British Waterways, not content with their spring onslaughts on the path itself, were now taking on the trees and shrubs. A certain amount of quite legitimate thinning had been done on the spindly sycamores and thorns, but also some indiscriminate felling of mature ash and hazel – which seemed a particularly cynical move on the eve of National Tree Planting Year. (I was later told that this burst of destructive energy was the result of a competition for the 'best-kept' section of towpath!)

It was a poor prospect for the few lone-wolf fieldfares and redwings, fresh in from Scandinavia, which were searching for winter food. This time last year the bushes had been swaying with their weight as they feasted off the berries. But there was still just enough fruit about to make a rough sort of chart of the weather and insect industry of the months past. Those neat parcels of nuts on the hazels came from a freak spell in March, two weeks of still, sunlit, frost-free days that cosseted the fragile female blooms from which the cobs grow. The sparse fruits on the sloes and hawthorns were a legacy of the damp and cold that had stretched through April and May. The summer had not been all fruitless gloom though: July had gone out in a blaze hot and dry enough to keep every fly drunk on wild rose nectar, and the bushes were heavy with hips as a result.

All along the cut creatures were acclimatising to the new season and the changing habitat. Wintering pied and grey wagtails, down from the north and west, were skitting about the rafts of weed and debris that had built up between the locks, using chunks of polystyrene as stepping-stones. Twice I glimpsed a water rail mincing furtively along the reedy edges of those cress beds that were still in use. The old pools which were now being dug out by the JCBs had been the traditional wintering site for our local rails. But having to evacuate to these new beds, which were raked out regularly by the cress farmers, did not seem to have perturbed them. They hadn't adapted to me though. The moment I broke cover they would scuttle back into the reeds like scared chickens.

There were a pair of dabchicks too, diving after sticklebacks. They spent more of their time under the water than on it, sometimes submerging for over fifteen seconds along the deep centre spine of the cut. I was able to follow their underwater progress by the arrowhead trace marks on the surface. They reminded me at first of miniature submarines, with their streamlined bodies and bullet heads; then, by an unnerving association, with the Nazi ducks (they manned their U-boats wearing those infamous green helmets above their surly bills) that had featured as the villains in a Dutch children's picture book I had been given for a wartime Christmas. I am resigned to the way these childhood images push into the limelight. The most resolute objectivity has no chance against those first vivid encounters with dolled-up fairy story animals.

But the best was yet to come. I had turned for home and was passing the last bank of willows before the canalside bungalows began. About a hundred yards ahead of me there was a sudden, clear splash at the edge of the water. Before I had time to speculate whether it was a leaping pike or a lobbed stone, there was another identical fountain in the same spot. It was a kingfisher. I walked on as patiently as I could until I was about twenty yards from the willow under which I'd seen the splashes. I scanned the tree through my field glasses, and within a few seconds the bird shot out, arcing across the water like a high voltage spark. He put down in another willow almost directly opposite me. With the brazen nerve of a stuntman he began swallow-diving for fish at the very edge of the cut, in water that because of the drought was no more than a few inches deep. Normally kingfishers take up look-out posts a few feet above the surface, arrow down almost vertically, submerge several inches and rocket out again a second or so later. If a bird had tried this technique here, he would have quickly suffered concussion. This kingfisher was diving from a branch not more than eighteen inches above the water, at an angle of nearly 45 degrees, and was using his wings as a brake so that he barely submerged at all.

Between plunges he would squat on the branch peering rather casually at the water. But at times he would cock his head and glare down with just one eye – perhaps to gain a more directly penetrating view of what lay beneath the water before sighting up with two. At other times he would spin through 180 degrees to squint at the water behind him, switching so fast between his russet front and the iridescent turquoise of his back that he seemed like one of those revolving metal targets on a fairground rifle range.

I saw kingfishers by the canal all that winter, whirring under the bridges, pacing the trains, and once (from a bus again), perched on a streamside post only twenty yards from a main road in the centre of a new town. And there was a memorable afternoon in early spring when I saw a pair rocketing and twisting through the tree tops in their courtship chase.

To a well-wrapped human with a fire and a hot meal to return to, there is something very lifting about a walk on a bright winter's day. The landscape seems stripped clean, pared back for the fight against the cold. But for the creatures that live there, the fight is no Christmas card fancy of fluffed-out feathers and shiny noses, but a real life-and-death struggle. It is then that the urban areas, with their warmer air, unfrozen water and food parcels handed out by kindly humans, become a real blessing. I could not count the number of times I have strode manfully out on winter days into an almost birdless landscape in the deep countryside, only to return and find the belt of bijou gardens I had left hours before brimming with birds. It's been estimated that during the terrible freeze-up of 1962/63, over a million birds were saved from starvation by the food provided by householders.

As much as anything it is the variety and concentration of food and shelter in gardens that makes them so attractive to struggling winter birds. Windfall apples – often barely covered by snow because of the shelter provided by fruit tree branches – will draw in fieldfares, redwings and mistle thrushes from the whited-out fields. Bullfinches will scrump buddleia seedheads, redpolls and linnets swing after birch catkins, and goldcrests dither like humming birds around the exotic conifers. Even kingfishers have been known to visit garden ponds and waterbutts in the heart of towns when the outlying lakes and rivers are frozen over. And if a garden has a nesting-box it will likely be put to as profitable a use on cold nights as in the breeding season. In the chill heart of the '62/63 winter over forty wrens were seen flying in to roost together in a single nesting-box in Norfolk. What can it have been like inside? Did the birds devise some selfless rota, changing places to share the warmth and stave off suffocation? There were apparently no corpses in the box in the morning.

It would be foolish to become too sentimental about this, and to see beneficent garden owners as the saviours of our wild birds. It is a hard fact of animal life that something like three out of four young birds do not survive their first year, whatever the weather. If they escape disease in the nest and being picked off by predators whilst they are still unsteady on their wings, then the chances are that they will die of starvation in their first winter. Birds live at what for us would be feverheat. A small bird burns up so much energy that he needs to eat as much as a third of his body weight a day just to stay alive – and in winter there is simply not enough food around to give every bird his iron rations.

Nor, when you think about it, could it be otherwise. If the majority of young birds survived to breed there would very quickly be a population explosion, with impossible territorial demands being made upon a countryside shrinking by the day, and a food crisis in the summer as well as the winter. A pair of great tits, for example – great garden haunters in the winter months – produce about ten eggs per clutch. If they kept this up, and all their offspring survived to breed at the same rate, then at the end of ten years there would be over 120 million tits where there had previously been only two. Each one would need to catch roughly 25 insects every minute of the winter day. It's clearly an impossible situation. Only the fittest – and the luckiest – young birds can survive. The rest must die at some time during the year whatever we do, to keep the population of each species at a level which can be supported by the available food, territories and nesting sites. But how the provision of scraps and special bird food can help is in preventing population crashes in areas where unnaturally severe conditions threaten to bring the population down *below* this level.

But the food which is both deliberately and unintentionally provided in gardens isn't of benefit only to the birds. The householder gets his reward too, in the shape of closer and more intimate views of bird behaviour than he can get in any other way. There are times in the winter when I find it almost impossible to write at home, so great is the distraction outside. My study window overlooks the lawn, and from Christmas onwards our small garden is crammed with greater numbers of more species than at any other time of the year. They are tamer, too – or at least more prepared to suspend their intolerance of man. They don't have much choice if they are to grab their share of the takings, and as a result you can watch, first-hand, the processes of adjustment to man-made facilities actually taking place.

We save our nut-bags until the first real freeze-up of the winter. Then they're hung out along the washing line about ten feet from the house. I have measured the time taken for the birds to discover the nuts after they are put up for the first time each winter. Invariably blue tits are the first to arrive, between twelve and fifteen minutes after I hang up the bag. Are these wily adult birds who know, by experience, a well-stocked larder when they see one? I have seen tits prospecting empty nut bags on a garden seat, which suggests that like well-conditioned consumers, they remember and recognise food by its packaging.

Once the blue tits have blazed the trail to the bags the other birds come crowding in: great tits diving on to the netting like Kamikaze pilots, sometimes with such gluttonous force that they knock their smaller cousins for six. There will likely be greenfinches as well, less dextrous but even more tetchy. If other birds come too close to them they shape up like heraldic emblems, beaks open, wings stretched and tails splayed to show their lime green outer feathers. But it is not a very serious threat display. It seems as if it has become an evolutionary advantage for birds to moderate their instinctive territorial aggression during the winter. There is certainly a good deal of sense in opting for a more co-operative lifestyle in the cold months; by sticking together and pooling experience, birds are more likely to be able to make best use of new-found food supplies and to get advance warning of predators.

Even blackbirds and robins, normally the most territorially jealous of garden birds, are prepared to drop their guard in the winter. It doesn't seem to put them at a disadvantage: urban blackbirds actually put on weight during the cold, whilst their country cousins are enduring an unwilling slimming regime that reduces their weight by an average of twenty percent. And just as many species in the open countryside form communal flocks in the winter, so they seem happy to rub wings on the nut bags. I have counted up to ten birds crowded on to a single bag, and as many as four species at once – greenfinches, and great, blue and coal tits.

Strung along the lilac and rose branches, queuing for a place, will be more tits. And underneath the bag itself, waiting for the crumbs, robins, dunnocks and house sparrows. But sparrows are amongst our most adaptable and successful birds, and they don't stay earthbound for long. After half an hour or so of watching the bespoke vertical feeders with their prehensile claws, the more ambitious sparrows are up having a try themselves.

The enterprise of birds in coping with the dark and cold is a marvel. Those same sparrows (and pied wagtails) have taken to feeding during the night shifts in factories – anything to boost the number of hours in which life-giving victuals can be soaked up. Birds who've learned to take advantage of our own insulations against time and season can become so nonchalant that I have seen a blackbird in full spring song under the arc lamps round a football pitch in the middle of December.

This is the time, too, when, with no nestlings clamouring for first-class protein, a tit turns its eyes most avariciously to the top of the milk. The extraordinary habit of mining open bottle tops to sip the cream is by all accounts a recent development. The first recorded case was in Hampshire in 1921, when tits were observed prising open the cardboard tops that were used then. By the end of the nineteen-forties the habit had spread throughout the country, and had been extended to the hammering of holes in metal foil tops. The fact that tits tend not to stray very far from their territories in the course of the year, and that not only other species of tit, but blackbirds, sparrows, starlings and robins have all begun excavating, suggests that the rapid spread of the habit was due to birds learning the trick from each other.

But why did they start in the first place? It is scarcely conceivable that those original tits had ever sampled cream, let alone learned to recognise it inside the confines of a milk bottle. The best answer is probably that tearing at cardboard is a natural part of tits' feeding activity in man-made surroundings. Once they had been unexpectedly rewarded by a beakful of cream, they quickly realised the existence of a new food source and began responding directly to the sight of a bottle.

The tearing of cardboard and paper seems to have a much longer history among the tit population. There is a delightful poem about paper-making, published in 1693, which describes somewhat ruefully the damage a tit can wreak:

> Small is this naughty Fowl, yet it can wreak
> No small destruction with its claws and beak.
> For, when paper from afar it spies,
> Straightway through open Window in it flies.
> Its frequent blows the sheets do quickly tear
> Still sodden, and make Havoc everywhere . . .
>
> from *Man and Birds* by R. K. Murton, 1971

No open window, it would seem, is sacrosanct to an inquisitive tit. A mob of twenty once invaded the chapel at Winchester College and began shredding the old books. Eric Hosking photographed one tit, obviously with ambitions to become a music-hall performer, tearing up a telephone directory. Many householders have discovered these birds ripping up wallpaper, peeling the stamps off letters and tearing down notices on parish hoardings.

There would seem to be two plausible explanations for this vandalism, which – until the birds discovered the virtues of the pinta milka – holds no apparent survival value for them. Firstly, that in winter, the whole of a tit's energy is devoted to exploring every conceivable food source. Secondly, that in areas where a good deal of artificial food is provided on a plate, so to speak, many tits find they can gorge themselves full in a fraction of the time it would take if they were hunting in the wild. They are left with a surplus of energy which, like footloose teenagers, they take out on any vaguely destructible object.

On the rubbish tips the chief winter opportunists are the gulls, which become out-and-out scavengers at this time of the year. They feed off scraps of old meat and bread that they root out from the garbage. Their foraging flocks are often hundreds strong, and are made up from as many as six species: black-headed, herring, greater black-backed, common, less black-backed, and just once in a while a solitary and ghostly glaucous gull from the Arctic. The birds don't spend their whole time at the tips. They roost on gravel pits and reservoirs at night, then flight out to their feeding grounds at tips, playing fields and even blocks of offices in the city centres, where they loiter about, hoping for sandwich remnants thrown from the windows.

I often wonder what an urban winter would be like without the gulls. There is so little real winter in a city, none of those pearl-white skies and fields of untramped snow of the open countryside. For five or six graceless months we stamp about with the sort of annoyance felt when the central heating goes wrong. Yet catch a glimpse of a line of gulls straggling home from their feeding grounds through the late afternoon mist, or squalling round the top of an office block, and suddenly winter becomes a season of the year again, a time of comings and goings, of a struggle for survival in conditions that our own style of life has muffled.

W. H. Hudson watched the wintering gulls over St James's Park, just about the time when they were beginning to change from being chiefly seaside birds to all-round urbanites:

> . . . on January 30, 1898, I passed by the water and saw
> the gulls there, where indeed they have spent most of the
> daylight hours since the first week in October. It was a rough
> wild morning; the hurrying masses of dark cloud cast a
> gloom below that was like twilight; and though there was no
> mist the trees and buildings surrounding the park appeared
> vague and distant. The water, too, looked strange, in its

intense blackness, which was not hidden by the silver-grey
light on the surface, for the surface was everywhere rent
and broken by the wind, showing the blackness beneath.
Some of the gulls – about 150 I thought – were on the water
together in a close flock, tailing off to a point, all with their
red beaks pointing one way to the gale. Seeing them thus,
sitting high as their manner is, tossed up and down with
the tumbling water, yet every bird keeping his place in the
company, their whiteness and buoyancy in that dark setting
was quite wonderful. It was a picture of black winter and
beautiful bird life which would have had a rare attraction
even in the desert places of the earth; in London it could not
be witnessed without a feeling of surprise and gratitude.

We see in this punctual return of the gulls, bringing their
young with them, that a new habit has been acquired, a
tradition formed, which has given to London a new and
exceedingly beautiful ornament, of more value than many
works of art.

Hudson saw all birds as extensions of the landscapes in which
they moved. For him, there was no more fitting place for a jackdaw
than toying in the wind above a church:

I have often thought that it was due to the presence of the
daw that I was ever able to get an adequate or satisfactory
idea of the beauty of some of our finest buildings. Watching
the bird in his aerial evolutions, now suspended motionless,
or rising and falling, then with half-closed wings precipitating
himself downwards, as if demented, through vast distances,
only to mount again with an exultant cry, to soar beyond
the highest tower or pinnacle, and seem at that height no
bigger than a swift in size – watching him thus, an image of
the structure over and around which he disported himself
so gloriously has been formed – its vastness, stability,

and perfect proportions – and has remained thereafter a vivid picture in my mind. How much would be lost to the sculptured west front of Wells Cathedral, the soaring spire of Salisbury, the noble roof and towers of York Minster and of Canterbury, if the jackdaws were not there!

Birds in London, 1898

Churches and churchyards are double-strength sanctuaries for wildlife. They provide a refuge not just because of their mature trees and stonework, but because even the most wily schoolboy nester would think twice before pinching jackdaws' eggs from under the sexton's nose. The age and continuity of use of churchyards also gives them a chance to build up stable communities of plants.

I've touched earlier on the swifts and kestrels that may nest in the spires in summer. In winter the role of the urban church as an unmolested island of stone crannies and ancient wood is just as vital. The church itself may be a hibernation site for a bat colony – which may indeed be in the belfry but more likely along the roof beams in the nave and side aisles. Church bat droppings have been known to liven up the most tedious of sermons, and, more seriously, damage brass and marble monuments. But bats are one of our most endangered classes of mammal. Their traditional roosting sites in hollow trees, old buildings and caves are being wiped out. Whole colonies are sometimes destroyed just on the strength of some ignorant superstitions, and some, quite shamefully, because so-called biologists are offering up to £20 a time for dissection specimens of the rarer species. So the importance of churches as sanctuaries for bats cannot be overestimated. Luckily the Church itself has recognised its Christian responsibility to the living creatures which take up residence in its buildings, and has recommended that every effort should be made to protect the bats.[*]

[*] See *Wildlife Conservation in the care of Churches and Churchyards,* Church of England Council for Social Responsibility, 1972.

The churchyard is likely to be the site of a number of old trees. Where these are indigenous British species like oak and elm, they may be the only mature hardwoods in the district. They will probably be visited by woodpeckers and owls, and may provide a site for a rookery. But the evergreens have their place too. Exotic firs and spruces give bed and board to tits and goldcrests. If there is a Wellingtonia, its spongy bark may attract treecreepers, which ferret out grubs with their curved, lockpicker's bills.

But it is the holly and the ivy and the yew that we think of first when we think of churchyards in the heart of winter. They are plants whose links with human festivals go back to before the Christian era. Holly, with its blood-red berries and vexingly sharp leaves standing firm against the frosts, was looked on as a tree of great power. Wreaths and garlands made from the branches were hung about dwellings to keep away goblins and witches. Ivy survives the cold, too, and having no real trunk of its own but twining enticingly round the boles of other trees became the feminine foil to holly's sharp and vivid masculinity. They slipped easily into Christian mythology, possessing between them a whole armoury of symbols. The red berries represented Christ's blood, the spiny branches His crown of thorns. Yet the blossom of holly was virgin white, rounding the life of this single plant into an allegory of Our Saviour's birth and passion – as surely as the black berries and serpentine coils of ivy represented the darker forces.

Like these, yew survives in churchyards despite its pagan ancestry. It was worshipped for its brooding dark presence – still the most dramatic contrast with grey stone to be found in the tree world – and for the strength suggested by its poisonous scarlet berries. It was a favourite wood for weapons as a result, lending its strength to the user. The most ancient wooden weapon ever found – a spear some seventy thousand years old – was made from yew. And many of the sacred sites where yews grew were converted along with their pagan worshippers.

When the early Christians were looking for boughs to spread before the processions on Palm Sunday, they turned naturally to the soft evergreen foliage which abounded round their churches at this early spring date, weeks before most trees had sprouted. Belief in the tree's magical powers survived Christianisation. It would ward off sickness and evil. The yew in my parish churchyard is cowled like some protective pall-cloth over the untitled burial mound of our town's plague victims. The yew tree, like the man-made ornaments in the church, is a monument of centuries of social history. Look at it and you are looking back beyond the raising of the church itself, to a time when belief in the supernatural was more fervent and fearful than we can ever imagine.

Yet the tree holds no fear for the birds. Mistle thrushes gobble up the berries, passing the poisonous central seed in their droppings. And here, where the limy patches have splashed on to the gravestones, another strange natural circle is joined. Not seedling yews, but rosettes of lichens take hold, whorls of orange and yellow and green like landlocked coral, nourished by the minerals in the droppings. Lichens are one of our most successful plant forms, yet are a frail working partnership between a rootless alga and a fungoid shell unable to manufacture its own foodstuffs. So the alga feeds the fungus, which pays its debt by anchoring the plant to surfaces where no plant with conventional roots could find a grip. They are compensated for their fragility by being the first plants able to colonise bare stone. In many urban areas churchyards are like inland cliffs, moraines of craggy headstones and slabs that may be the only old stone in the district. And just as many plants of stony places like wall-pepper, pellitory-of-the-wall and ivy-leaved toadflax can find a home in the fissures of a church wall, so cliff-side mosses and lichens are able to colonise the face of the stonework. They have no seasons like flowering plants. When there is plenty of nutrient-rich moisture trickling down the stones they are able to grow. When it is dry they pass into a kind of petrified hibernation.

Lichens are exceptionally beautiful plants, even in longshot, before you see the innermost crystalline structure and the cups and caps sprouting out of the fungoid armour. They're responsible for much of the patina of old buildings, softening the sheerness of the surfaces and the uniformity of colour and texture.

But why only old buildings? Why don't lichens also brighten the concrete walls of office blocks and high-rise flats? It's true that on these more brutally functional buildings lichens are sometimes removed as dirty and corrosive. Yet it is not these tiny plants which are responsible for damaging urban stonework. Sulphur dioxide from industrial fumes is the real culprit. In a canny double-fronted attack it not only dissolves concrete and limestone, but effectively prevents most lichens from gaining a hold and hiding the scars.

Lichens are highly sensitive to pollution. Only one species – a plant called *Lecanora dispersa* which grows like a mat of tiny pebbles – will tolerate the very centre of cities. Farther out there may be powdery patches of lime-green *Caloplaca citrina*, yellow *Lecidea lucidae* and orange scales of *Xanthoria parietia*. It seems that other lichens cannot colonise stones which are already drenched with the sulphurous rain in industrial areas. (This is one reason why limestone blocks, which partially neutralise the acids, are such popular lichen sites.)

It is in the graveyard itself that the most poignant consequence of this sensitivity lies. The newer headstones, put up since the Industrial Revolution, are barren of these tempering, pioneer plants. The older stones, where lichens were able to establish their roothold before the rain became saturated with sulphurous acid, carry them to just the extent they had grown to before the atmosphere became intolerable. The lichens linger in isolation on these ancient stones, unable to colonise the new, date-stamped memorially like museum specimens as reminders of our thoughtlessness.

In the gravel pits and reservoirs a new group of visitors had moved in. Ducks fleeing from the harsh freeze-ups in Northern Europe love these comparatively warm and sheltered urban waters. They will even come into the very heart of cities to find them. There are two small reservoirs in Stoke Newington, less than four miles north of St Paul's, that by mid-winter often have a higher density of wildfowl than any other inland waters in the South of England. If the temperature begins to drop below freezing, this is the last surface to ice over, and the tufted duck from Iceland and pochard from Siberia can number literally thousands.

It is an extraordinary situation. These refugees from some of the wildest areas of Europe have homed in on a city lake no bigger than the Serpentine, that, almost completely surrounded by blocks of flats, looks like nothing so much as a large boating pond.

I envy the view of those who live in the upper flats. Non-residents like myself have to be content with peering embarrassedly through the chinks in the fence that cuts you off from this reservoir as securely as if you were in a prison compound. I have tried working round the perimeter of the reservoir, stealing into private forecourts and tiptoeing on garden walls for a better view, but the Metropolitan Water Board's barricade is impenetrable. You can always see the abundant ducks, and the rafts of coot and scattered grebes through the cracks; they are everywhere. But rarely the star guests at this reservoir, the smew that arrive early in the new year. There is no duck to approach the startling and sharp beauty of this vagrant from the Arctic. The old wildfowlers used to call it the white nun, from the pure black and white plumage of the drake. The reservoirs in the London area are the winter stronghold of this duck. The Stoke Newington reservoirs alone have been known to hold flocks of over thirty.

A good number, but not enough to guarantee a glimpse through that forbidding fence. Such a small piece of engineering could do so much to cheer this bleak corner of London.

The pits that run down the Colne Valley have no such barriers. I walked the length of them on one of those blissful early March days that are just about all we see of spring nowadays. The temperature was up in the sixties and a breeze was blowing in from the south-west, yet within three weeks it was sleeting again.

But premature and deceptive though the weather may have been, the birds weren't showing any signs of being prudent. With a joyous indifference to what they were, and where they were supposed to breed, they were responding to the immemorial biochemical changes sparked off by the light and warmth and hurling themselves into their courtship displays. Gulls somersaulted in the air. A pair of kestrels spiralled above the fresh gravel quarries. Grebes, now back in their ruffs, slid towards each other like alligators. A male goldeneye, surrounded by five doting ducks, bashed his triangular head back onto his liquorice-striped body. He might have been getting them worked up by these antics, but they would be five-hundred miles north-east of this temporarily benign pit before they got down to breeding in earnest.

There was much else besides. A red-crested pochard, a rare vagrant from Eastern Europe with a bill so luridly crimson that it looks like Bakelite. A solitary cormorant overhead, as dark and reptilian as a pterodactyl. Kingfishers, siskins, herons, teal.

At times like this I would find in myself an affection for these grubby landscapes that I could never have predicted and would be hard put to excuse. Visually, they were without exception ugly. Although the healing processes of natural growth were everywhere in evidence (they were what I had been looking at the whole year), each one of these habitats represented an assault upon some green country. They had none of the restful predictability of ancient countryside, that feeling of seasoned flow and stability that you find in downland and forest.

Yet it is the disorder and incongruity that I find so exciting and irresistible. These are the last 400 yards of my walk, which has become a favourite stretch. It begins, in characteristic metaphorical style, with two signs: the nameplate of a demolition company, and one of those bottle-green bridleway signposts. A real touch of the hunting shires inside the muck-tip belt; there is even a practice jump fifty yards on, where a drainage hose from a used car dump lopes across the path!

You cannot stride about in surroundings like this. Every step can produce something which, by rights, shouldn't be there. To the right of the track there is the steep bank of a vast rubbish tip. It's clothed, as you might expect, with coltsfoot and the shoots of tantalisingly unidentifiable aliens. But there are also forget-me-nots, and at the bottom of the bank, water parsnip and yellow iris. The source of these damp-loving plants lies to the left of the track, a still-worked pit where I have seen common terns diving for fish in May. There is an abandoned bomb-shelter, veloured with moss; mounds of cans and rubble where robins nest despite the rats. Best of all I like the bridge at the end of the track, built vertiginously out of a collection of scaffolding tubes and wire hawsers.

It leads you back over a channel between two pits to a promontory made up from overgrown gravel heaps. The folds between them are like miniaturised Dorset coombes, flanked with bramble and blackthorn that bristle with whitethroats through the summer.

There are mature trees too, especially a fine clump of alders. On that early March day a flock of a dozen siskins were skirmishing through them, singing occasionally the endearing jumble of twitters and creaks that once made them popular as cage-birds, and plucking the seeds from the alder cones. And even here, in this cluttered landscape, the cycles go on: in the damp mould under the alders were the tiny cups of *Ciboria amentacea*, an exquisite fungus that grows on the previous year's fallen catkins.

174

But I'd deceived myself too easily. Change may produce some spectacular variety, but it also exacts a price. When I went back along this track a few weeks later, the alder clump had vanished, bulldozed down for an anglers' car park and buried underneath the demolition company's rubble.

This was the day I was collared by the owner of the pits. They were private property it seemed, for fishermen only. Still, he ejected me very amicably, and we chatted for a while about the luxuriance of this spot. He was genuinely concerned to foster its wildlife – the fish-hungry grebes excepted. He took me to see an old willow (which had barely survived the bulldozers' onslaughts), where a mallard had tried to nest. He explained how one day the eggs had been stolen. He was sure it was schoolboy 'vandals' invading his territory from the bridleway. 'And we built that earth bank to keep them out' he mourned. He waved his hand, past the half-shattered tree, across the car park to the ridge where the rubble had been piled up over the alder roots, oblivious to the example of legalised destruction he had set.

There is a limit to the recuperative powers of the natural world. It will always fight back, but it cannot survive outright eradication, as I was to be reminded a few months later. It was late June, and I had tracked down that ruined farm that Orwell had written his poem from, hoping that, forty years later, it would have proved his pessimism unjustified. But it was a crumbling and dejected place, beaten back by the sheer weight of development crowding in on it. There were a few strips of vegetables, but most of the ground had been occupied by used-car dumps and football pitches. There were scarcely any trees remaining and the chief vegetation above grass level was a few clumps of elder and hawthorn. That these bushes would soon be draped, not with an honest English climber like traveller's joy, but with the extravagant trumpet blossoms of an alien bindweed, the American bellbine, would not, I think, have reassured Orwell. This hardy immigrant would live on, I guess, and some greenery continue to brighten this bleak industrial landscape. But it was not the set-piece I was looking for. The odds were too one-sided. Even the factories themselves once 'white and clear/Like distant glittering cities . . .' were now dark with grime and age.

I ended up at an abandoned brickyard at the very edge of my chosen area. I suppose that it had ceased to be used about three years before, and it was now a dumping ground for any household rubbish too big for the bin. But successive excavations of the sand and clay for the bricks had left the yard with a legacy of mature waste ground. The abandoned mounds were thick with wild rose, hawthorn and the young shoots of rosebay. The steep-sided pits had filled with water, and though they had little or no vegetation in them, they were buzzing with water boatmen, diving beetles and newts. And the paths between, once heavily-used tracks over the light soil, carried one of the most brilliant collections of dry-soil flowers I have ever seen: ox-eye daisies, centauries, vetches, late cowslips, lady's bedstraw, musk mallow knee-high.

What a place it would be for children! They could dip in the ponds, rummage through the piles of old wartime haversacks, and pick flowers to their heart's content – it would make no difference to the abundance of this place. But I doubt if they will get the chance. Such a desirable area of vacant ground, right on the edge of an expensive residential estate, will not stay as wasteland for long. It might be saved by being designated as a nature reserve (it is rich enough) and be improved into the bargain.

But I must confess that I cherish the hope that it will live out what little time is left to it unmolested by any humans, naturalists or not. They might keep the scrub back and introduce water-weeds to the ponds, but I fear they would lose the place its sense of wonder and surprise. Not many planned reserves could re-create the feeling of coming upon this place by accident: through the 'executive villas', under the iron gate, past the crumbling brick ovens, already vanishing under the rosebay, and on to this tangle of wildness, with Welsh poppies and teasels growing out of the mounds of bricks and broken glass.

I walked to the very edge of the yard. There was one of the deepest pits here and into it had been pushed and abandoned a saloon car. The air and weather had already begun to get hold of it. The bodywork was rusting and the rubber beginning to peel off the tyres.

But there were more miraculous healing forces at work. Sidling over the bonnet and poking through the hole where the windscreen had been, were sweep upon sweep of spotted orchid, in every shade of pink. This most delicate of flowers, hounded by new roads and car-borne trippers, had found refuge amongst the clutter, and was having its revenge.

Acknowledgements

My belated thanks to all my colleagues at Penguin Education who accompanied me on my forays around the West Middlesex badlands. And today, my deep gratitude to Adrian and Gracie Cooper, and Little Toller, for their support, trust and enterprise in bringing out this new edition, almost half a century after the first.

R. M.

Norfolk, 2021

The Richard Mabey Library

When Little Toller Books started its publishing journey in 2008, Richard Mabey was among the very first authors we invited to help us re-issue the classics of nature writing and rural life in the British Isles. He suggested writing a new introduction to Richard Jefferies' *Wild Life in a Southern County*, which, aged 12, was his first encounter with nature writing. 'When I found my elder sister's copy, I was mesmerised. Here were thoughts about how animals might think, and how landscapes made you feel.'

Shortly after working with Richard on *Wild Life*, we started discussing his own book, *The Unofficial Countryside*, which had fallen out of print. Although it was originally published in 1973, well ahead of its time and before either of the founders of Little Toller were even born, when *Unofficial* was reissued in 2010 it transformed Little Toller's purpose and reach. The timing of the reissue also marked the beginnings of a wider resurgence in nature writing across the UK, and the book has remained in print with us ever since. But much more than demonstrating the appetite of the British book-reading public, *Unofficial* defined for us the truer meaning of 'classic' as something with enduring originality and relevance.

Over the last 50 years, regardless of where publishing fashions were at, Richard has remained committed and absolutely focussed on exploring the relationship between nature and culture, and his thinking in these books continues to inspire across the generations. This body of work continues to shape our publishing story, too, and during his eightieth year, The Richard Mabey Library celebrates the depth and range of his writing life. It is also our way of thanking him for the support and nurture he has given Little Toller over the years.

We start The Richard Mabey Library with *Nature Cure*, *The Unofficial Countryside*, *Gilbert White* and *Beechcombings*. All these books will be hardback, printed in Cornwall, and feature original artwork by Michael Kirkman. For the type, we have returned to Sabon, designed by the German-born typographer and designer Jan Tschichold, and which Little Toller used for all its early books. To find out more about the other titles in The Richard Mabey Library, please get in touch.

Little Toller Books

w. littletoller.co.uk E. books@littletoller.co.uk